Argyll

The Enduring Heartland

Argyll

The Enduring Heartland

SECOND EDITION
Revised by the Author

Colin Baxter Photography, Grantown-on-Spey, Scotland

First published in Great Britain 1977

This edition published 1995 by
Colin Baxter Photography Ltd,
Grantown-on-Spey,
Morayshire,
Scotland, PH26 3NA

A CIP catalogue record for this book is available from the British Library

ISBN 0-948661-64-X

Printed in Great Britain by The Cromwell Press

Cover Photograph: CASTLE STALKER, APPIN, ARGYLL

Contents

Contents

Remember Well

John Campbell of Kilberry (1873-1928)
Linguist, Soldier, Poet;
Marion Isabel Durand (1881-1945)
Musician and Painter

and Mary (1917-1995)

Gus am bris an Là

Introduction

THIS IS a book about my home-ground.

I wanted to call it *My Argyll*, because that is what it is – one person's understanding of past and present, one idea for the future – but the title sounded too selfish for a book that sets out to share, welcome, explain, introduce a beloved landscape to new friends.

Argyll has changed its shape more than once within my own lifetime, extending from the Clyde to the farthest westerly tip of Britain and from the Mull of Kintyre to Loch Shiel, or shrinking south-eastwards even as it stretched to take in Bute. Such things have come and gone in other times, seldom altering the feeling of people for their own corner.

I must at once apologise for neglecting some corners and some cherished traditions. A book such as this can only – must only – reflect a personal view; besides, there are many places in this wide territory that I have never seen, islands unvisited, hills I shall not climb now. I defend myself with a phrase from Donnchadh Bàn MacIntyre our poet – *chan fhaca tusa i leis na suilean agamsa*; you have not seen her with my eyes.

And now I confront you with a Gaelic phrase. For that I make no apology. This is a bilingual country still, and in childhood I had the freedom of two tongues. Gaelic has every right to grace a book on Argyll.

Here, then, is what I have learnt about my home, from books or from friends or dredged from my blood and heritage. I have taken places and events to illustrate each other, and have tried to explain why we are as we are, what you can expect of us and what we desire for ourselves. This is not a professional historian's or sociologist's study but the thoughts of a native woman, a voice from the inside like those that now sound out from other distant corners; shoots from an old rootstock that has struck again in many soils, but still blooms at home.

If you want to use this volume as a guidebook, I suggest you work from the index where you will find many of the placenames and a rough indication of how to pronounce them. If you prefer to take the chapters as they come, you will find them set in chronological order.

I owe thanks to all the friends who have shared their knowledge with me all my days, and those who gave unstinting help in the writing – especially the staff of the District Library. I am grateful for permission to quote from published works: to Mrs M O Anderson and Messrs Nelson, for extracts from *Adomnan's Life of Columba*; to the late Sir James Fergusson for quotations from *The White Hind*; to Mrs Bratton and the Neil Munro Trust for *John o'Lorn* and extracts from *The New Road* and *Para Handy*; and to the late George Campbell Hay for generous leave to use his own poems and to quote from *Gillespie* by the late Revd J MacDougall Hay, his father. I can never begin to thank Mary Sandeman for a lifetime's friendship.

Returning to a project after seventeen years is daunting. I have moved house, by a few yards; perhaps my viewpoint has also changed. At least I can correct some blunders that have long irked me, and take note of some new discoveries. The first edition had extensive notes and a large bibliography, both now rather outdated; I have taken the former into the text and pruned the latter. For this fresh opportunity I must particularly thank my friend Jim Crumley, for suggesting the reprint to his publisher Colin Baxter; I am grateful to Mike Rensner for much sympathetic editorial help.

The changes are, I hope, for the better; the errors are all still my own work. One at least is deliberate; one can hardly describe artforms, language, customs, laws and myths as 'pertaining to ethnic groups at sundry times inhabiting parts of Switzerland, France, England, Wales, Cornwall, Ireland and Scotland and sharing some of these characteristics with other groups elsewhere'; well, not every time. I am well aware that 'Celtic', with a hard 'C', is a linguistic and not an ethnic term; but it will have to serve.

Don't let the Gaelic words frighten you; they are not as difficult as they are made to look by a standard spelling devised by bygone pedants, mostly non-Gaels. As for Scots words, take a run at them and mutter them aloud; they are no more difficult than English dialects.

In this part of Argyll our expression for 'thank you' is *gun robh math agaibh* – may it be pleasant to you; I hope it is.

Kilberry, 1995

ARGYLL
The Enduring Heartland

Taigh na Ghlinne

Cathadh sneachd aig ceann na ghlinne,
Mór an t-uisge anns an t-sruth;
Glè-dhealrach òr na conaisge,
Glè-ghorm an speur.

Creagan dubha aig bun na ghlinne,
's eigheadail an t-eas;
Cuithean tearc ann an doire,
's an smùid sàmhach deas.

Glè-shàmhach anns a'ghleann,
Sàmhchair aig mo chrìdhe;
Caoimhneil mo thaighs' am measg nan conasg,
Fo'n speuran's chuantan ghorma.

The Glen House

The snow lies at the head of the glen,
The burn is running high;
Very bright is the gold of the whins
And very blue the sky.

The rocks are black at the foot of the glen
and ice-bright at the fall;
Strange and few are the drifts in the whins;
The still smoke is tall.

Very calm is the air in the glen,
Calm is the heart in me;
Warm is my house in the place of the whins
With the blue on the sky and the sea.

Kilberry, 1950 and 1973

1

Landscape with Figure

IT IS very early on a summer's day.

Last night a saffron band lay along the northern ridge at midnight, heat-heavy leaves drooping black against it under a faint star. Westward and seaward the tide fetched in the haze until a white mist hid the water. Now the mist has rolled, heavy as the pulled locks of fleeces, over the white sand where the terns drowse; it has coiled above the machair and eased the small herbs' thirst; it has filled every gully and billowed up the steep face of the grass cliff. Below the fenced edge of the field it spreads in a level carpet. It hides the sea, letting only a fret and a whisper rise through the blanket from which erupt the sleepy heads of islands.

At the inland side of the field a gate opens. A man leaves the trees for the open ground.

The mist has hidden the hayfields and veiled the deep green of growing corn. The cattle are up on the rough parks, the sheep lie cudding their dawn feed. The only animal afoot is this one, treading the dew-wet grass.

As he walks steadily to the headland a gull drifts above him, a redshank pipes from the hidden shore, a pair of curlews float from the hill with that *Tui-tui...tui-tui-tui* that wrenches the exiled heart. Man and birds are thirled to the turning tide, and they go now to seek their livelihood.

The tide itself once washed where now the mist lies, at the lip of a shelf carved by cold seas out of glacial drift, in that long age when land and sea played a slow see-saw and the rocks escaped from their vast ice-coffins. That was before the hunters came north and westwards from the lands where their far ancestors had caught Rhone salmon or chased the wild bulls of Altamira.

When the first man trod this ground is still an unanswered question; perhaps he came towing a sledge and hooded in deerskin to fish among the floes where the fat shoals swam; perhaps he traversed bleak tundra from pocket to stunted pocket of scrub-willow; perhaps already he braved the open sea.

Whenever he came, it was a while back even as rocks and sea count time – ten thousand years or so, give or take a summer. The sea had carved caves in the rocks above the newly lowered shoreline and left them neatly paved with storm-laid cobbles. There he could camp, or he could rig on the short turf of the sandy machair his rounded tent of skins.

They knew no abiding city, these firstcomers, nor could they have borne a fixed abode. It was in their hard-won skills to move with their food-supply, following deer to the narrow pass and seals to the breeding-reef, gulls to the loch and fish to the shallows. At a rich hunting-ground they might team with another band to cull whatever plenty was there; in lean times they must scatter far afield and make the best of anything they could find.

The seasons returned them to favoured camps, to add to last year's heap of shells and clean-picked bones, or to a sheltered cave with its spalls of worked flint on the sunny side of the entrance. They were themselves the rarest animals in their environment – many a brown bear and many a stag lived out its days without once snuffing the taint of woodsmoke.

Neat-footed, deft-handed, makers of the smallest of stone tools to arm their antler harpoons, they have not left us even the bones of their dead to show their stature (let alone their skin colour); as for the rich store of custom and ritual that most hunting-peoples use, that is gone beyond recall. We who like to fancy ourselves masters of the world should stop to wonder how we would fare in a trackless country, where the only food that did not see and hear better, and run faster, than we could, would be clammy shellfish and such plants or nuts as we could risk eating.

It's a skilful business, the really simple life, and most of us have lost the skills, though some basic thoughts remain. The control of man by his environment – not the other way about – is something the Gael remembers. His words for land and people are interchangeable, and he will tell you he 'belongs' to Skye or Islay or Knapdale; he, or his grandparents, may have left the home-ground, he may have been born in Glasgow or Toronto, but the bond holds fast.

Watch the sheep. They live on the heather, four or five acres of moorland to every ewe. We round them up and drive them to the fank for dipping and clipping and dosing for their manifold ills – many a harassed farmer thinks they spend their leisure dreaming up new diseases – but you will not see us driving them back to the hill. A gate is opened, a dog called to heel, and out trots the first old ewe. A white woolly ribbon of her sisterhood forms up behind her and unwinds towards the braeface; six turn along the ridge, five ford the burn, eight head for the pass...long before twilight each of them will be back in her own chosen place. She will drop her lamb, most likely, at the rock where she was lambed; if you offer her an easy old age in a lush pasture, she will butt and scramble her way home to ensure its birthright for her last lamb. She is "hefted to that hirsel", as we say, and the Gael is hefted too.

We are not the masters. The land dictates its use to all but the stubbornest of men, and most of all in hill-country where the sea has bitten deep. Here, and here only, can one cross the ridges; here is the ford; there a boat will lie safely on good holding-ground.

When the ice-fed sea was highest it made a bay of Crinan Moss and an inlet of Glassary Glen; Knapdale was an island, Kintyre another. The eighteenth-century droveroads followed ancient trackways marked by standing-stones, and the feet of travelling men turned aside to cool springs long before, and long after, the wells were guarded by rock-cut crosses. Man uses what he can find, but the skill is in the finding.

And now that solitary figure has crossed the field and vanished into the thinning mist. An engine putters into life; presently the boat appears, far out in a clear patch of sea, a narrow shape piled high with lobster-creels. Or are they creels, and is there an engine? Is it not some lean dark hull that brings old fears to land, or the curach of an Irish saint, or even a sealskin-and-whalebone kayak bearing the first bold seafarer?

The curlews might know, but they are busy on the tidewrack. Two gulls attend the boat – they know. The rabbits have come out on the machair as it warms under the sunrise, but it is no good asking them – they are Johnny-come-latelies with less than two hundred years to their credit or discredit.

And as for me, I can only tell it as I saw it, on a summer's morning, very early.

2

A Line of Footprints

TO UNDERSTAND a landscape one must learn its bones. Rock-gorge and flood plain, ice-smoothed hill or upthrust ridge record the earth's experience like wrinkles on an old face. A glance at the map discloses the skeleton of Argyll lying aslant from north-east to south-west, fingers of water probing along the joints. The slanting pattern predominates despite a multitude of basalt dykes that cut across it, signposts to ancient volcanoes. Our biggest hills are only the ghosts of mountains, stumps ground down from Andean heights by winds and millennial rains and the inexorable ice. Lochs fill the bottoms of old gulfs, the steps and benches of older shores streaking the hillsides above them, rivers run threadlike in grooves carved by glaciers, the peat grows quietly over ten thousand years of airborne seeds and the roots of drowned trees.

Most of our rocks are grey – silvery schists, dark diorite, greenish slates and bluish claystone, black lava. There are a few rosy outcrops of sandstone and granite, and everywhere the white sparkling quartz. Square miles of desolation cover the Moor of Rannoch, where the last ice harboured, crept outward, or shrank to hoard its cold. Neil Munro, in *The New Road*, caught the essence of Rannoch:

> The inn stood on a desert edge; behind rose up the scowling mountains of Glen Coe, so high and steep that even heather failed them, and their gullies sent down streams of stones instead of foam. Eastward the moor stretched flat and naked as a Sound; three days' march from end to end they said were on it – all untracked and desert-melancholy. Its nearer parts were green with boggy grass, on which the cannoch-tuft – the cotton-sedge – was strewn like flakes of snow; distantly its hue was sombre – grey like ashes, blackened here and there with holes of peat. The end of it was lost in mist from which there jutted, like a skerry of the sea,

Schiehallion. God-forgotten, man-forsworn, wild Rannoch, with the birds above it screaming, was the oddest thing, the eeriest in nature, he had ever seen.

The ice from Rannoch and the mountain-tops gouged out lochs and valleys as it found ways to the sea through rocks weakened by old earth-shifts or split by the frosts of centuries. Loch Awe sent its first green ice-fed waters out by Glassary; as the lake-level fell, the outflow coursed through the Eurach gorge to Kilmartin, laying down and slicing through deep gravel-terraces. Lastly the loch carved a door in Cruachan's flank and a new river thundered into Loch Etive.

A great rift-valley splits Scotland from Inverness to Islay; a lesser rift holds the string of lochs and passes from Dalmally to the sources of the Tay. These awesome cracks, and others buried deep beneath the soil, are still earthquake-conductors, so that Jura and Knapdale quiver when disaster hits an Ayrshire explosive-factory, and odd tremors come to rattle plates in lonely houses on a windless day.

The underground bones control the growth above, the green skin of earth revealing what lies below. Pine, oak and crouching juniper mark the change of soils, rare fern or common weed carry the message upward from their roots. The pulse of this body is the flow of waters, from the long sighing wave of tide-turn to the highest cold spring among the brilliant moss-tufts. Pelting watercourses and a dipper's chuckle; hill-lochs ringing to a diver's mad laughter; black peat-wallows for the roaring stag, muddy dubs for migrant waders, all are interlocked as closely as the plaitwork on carved stones.

Threaded through the landscape are the marks of men. High white hydro-electric dams and lines of spidery pylons on hillsides, roads winding along loch shores, little towns or isolated farmsteads, these are the works of a century or two. High above the roads lie the broad scars of droveways where once the cattle moved by thousands from Mull or Islay to Kilmichael Tryst, from Kilmichael to Crieff or Falkirk; here a hill-track bends to pass a cairn, there a standing-stone beckons the traveller towards a pass.

Up in the hills where the deer-grass ripples and an eagle's shadow races over it, everything is quiet and empty and unchanging – or so one thinks, until in some dark peatslip one sees white slivers of flint-chips or, eight feet into the ground, the bony roots of ancient pines. At the next shoulder the blue field of the Atlantic stretches out, for in Argyll the sea is never far away. Indeed, when the flocks and herds of Britain were ordered to be driven twelve miles inland under the threat of Napoleon's invasion, this was one county that could not obey, for nowhere in Argyll is there land so far from salt water.

Behind the newest bungalow, the prick-eared dormers of a farmhouse; behind the farm, the thick walls of a tin-roofed shed, once a thatched dwelling. Beside the square kirk, the medieval crucifix stands defaced but not cast down. Overlooking the castle or sealed beneath its foundations lie traces of an earlier fort. Across the face of the land goes a line of footprints leading back to our beginnings.

It can be hard to picture the length of that trail. "The Old Days" could mean the last century, or 1745 or Bruce-and-Wallace; it's all behind us and our eyes are on the road ahead. Yet the road would not be there, nor we on it, if travelling feet had not marked out its track. Here has been no clearcut break by Roman or Saxon, to displace all things old; invasions we have known, newcomers we accept, but Argyll has never yet undergone total exodus and resettlement.

This can make it harder to grasp the extent of our past, for lack of any line ruled across the account. Continuing custom blurs the picture; we forget that some relics were as much a mystery to our recent forebears as to ourselves, arousing curiosity and feeding fireside stories. Even volcanic bubbles in rocks on the north shore of Loch Crinan were explained as the hoofprints of Scota-the-daughter-of-Pharaoh's horse, bearing, as Nennius asserts, Jacob's pillow itself to be the Stone of Destiny and throne of future kings.

Customs endure. A century ago the Colonsay fishermen camped every summer in the great western caves of Jura, handy for the lobster-fishing which became worthwhile once a steamer-service could hurry the catch to market. Formerly the fishermen worked with lines and nets, earlier still with harpoons, visiting Jura when shed antlers could be found. These caves remain unexcavated, their mouths embanked and nettle-covered behind the stormbeach. Their lowest levels may well hold stone and antler tools matching those from Colonsay and Oronsay shell-mounds.

Shadowy migrants exploring the resources of the post-glacial sea were the first colonists of this ice-carved, rock-framed landscape. For maybe five thousand years their hunting bands roamed, learning every cliff and reef, every source of food or tools. When at last they saw a strange boat entering their bay, think how they must have crouched and whispered.

A biggish boat, deep-laden – they'll have waited for a quiet day; two-three men, women, children, sacks and bundles and – look at that, now! – two wee dumpy hand-tame beasts, smaller than roe deer, starting to graze as soon as they're steered to the grass; and (keep down, children!) a thing coming dripping up the shore, horns on her like Bull-of-the-Woods himself. So that's what they were towing – I couldn't make it out – that'll be its child they're lifting out of the nest at the stern. Well! Wait here, quietly now, while I go down and make peace-signs.

In a moon or two a hunter's child will offer a herdboy a string of fish and the boy's mother will send him back with a bowl of milk. Presently the boys will prance and wrestle and roll together on the grass, and their fathers will sit down laughing and study each other's spears. The farmer asks in sign-language where the hunter got that good flint; later the hunter will bring back an extra lump and exchange it for a cheese. His womenfolk warn the stranger children away from poisonous fruits, show off their babies and discuss the rival merits of fur cloaks and woven smocks.

Neither group is large enough to crowd the other, though the hunters cannot like the felling and burning, and the farmers are outraged when men and dogs stream across their new gardens. In time, and they have all the time in the world, they draw together; the ever-adaptable hunters sow seeds, the farmers turn to a bit of hunting as the cleared ground loses fertility. It is highly possible that some hunters already managed some red deer herds.

The farmers' remote origins lay far across Europe; they had moved westward, slowly as cattle move and crops ripen, generation by generation with seed-corn and livestock developed in distant lands, and rituals to ensure fertility. Their chief monuments today are big stone tombs. Whether these were communal for a kinship, or reserved for privileged chiefs, is unknown, nor can we tell if they were built grudgingly by slaves or raised in proud mourning by free men. Elsewhere these large graves may be earthen mounds concealing timber mortuaries; here they are of stone. Some lie like stranded whales by the shore, others on hillcrests, watching over the pastures. Often their entrances face the sunrise and a distant peak, as though the sleepers within should wake to the hills at dawn. The strength and skill that quarried huge slabs, sledged them into place and levered them upright, and the many hands that filled baskets and piled cobbles, still stir our imagination with hints of lost devotion.

After some centuries came rumour of approaching strangers who at last appeared – foreign in every way, appearance, dress, smell – carrying odd little red axes, and knives as sharp as flint. Daftlike folk, they wandered the hillsides scrabbling at rocks, exclaiming over patches of lichen; but with their discovery of the Crinan Lode, running from Craignish to Loch Fyne, the area burst into prosperity such as it has seldom enjoyed since. As the newcomers got down to their mining and smelting and casting, they too were absorbed into the community, even burying their dead within the stone mortuaries or, if they built their own round cairns, aligning them with the older structures. As their craft developed from simple coppersmithing to bronze-working, they needed all manner of goods; tin from Ireland or Cornwall to make bronze; beeswax for castings; amber, jet or cannel-coal for the magical amulets to gather filings by friction-induced static electricity. It would be the footloose sons of hunters who met these needs; they thought nothing of slipping across to Ireland or trekking through the hills with loads lighter than a dead deer. They had always attended gatherings, massive salmon-fishings, deerhunts, goose-drives, with rituals, all-night dancings, and the exchange of ceremonial gifts. Axe-stone from Antrim or Killin, flint from Mull and Ireland, changed hands at such meetings; if the new men offered good tools for barter, the elders would ensure their boys fetched whatever was wanted in return.

I can't see why it should be difficult to accept that these people were something more than shambling oafs. They are separated from us by some five thousand years and from the ape-men by nearer two million. Their ancestors survived the last Ice Age by their skilled endurance; the hunters developed high intelligence and excellent memory, the early farmers had tamed wild sheep and cattle in distant places, and improved wild grasses into grain. The hunters' women made baskets and fishtraps, cured and sewed skins for clothing (forget the cartoonists' beloved fur hearthrugs, think of Inuit boots and parkas); the settled women span and wove and made pottery (of little use among the travellers). The bronzesmiths produced tools still sharp enough to use when you are lucky enough to find one. Between them, they kept alive ancient skills and tackled communal tasks, all without a single textbook.

Herdsmen count flocks, women count weaving threads, bronzesmiths reckon weight and volume. Numeracy is older than literacy. To be illiterate does not imply stupidity but demands an efficient memory bank. A modern mathematician has proposed a deeply skilled geometrical construction for stone-settings.

Ever since the art of erecting them was lost, standing-stones have awed us. Legends surround them, of giants tossing them across lochs, witches spilling them in mid-flight, Sunday dancers frozen; all unknown to us housefast people, the Tinkers revere them and cherish their protection – as *The Horsieman* reveals (Williamson, Duncan, *The Horsieman: Memories of a Traveller 1928-1958*, Canongate, 1994). There they stand in rings or rows, in gossiping clumps or lonely dignity; now we glimpse the calculations that dictated their placement. I like to imagine the Advisory Group – of learned priests, of mathematical geniuses? – who drew plans on the earth and supervised the workforce, and then settled among their achievements to await moonrise, cracking their donnish jokes over the campfire. The stones remember but we have lost the zest of them.

Some could predict a lunar eclipse; some mark midwinter or the equinoxes – matters of deep concern to farming communities. Some now bear a Christian cross; others are pitted with dints as old as themselves, pecked out while the quarry-sap was in the stone as it lay.

Some dints are no larger than the broad end of an egg, others as big as a soup-plate; we call them 'cupmarks', sometimes 'cup-and-rings' when they are elaborated. They appear worldwide on suitable rock; some alongside Neanderthal graves; others made within living memory for a Zulu herdboy's gaming board. Hereabouts they cluster on rock-scalps and boulders, on the tall stones and within graves; some surrounded by concentric rings linked by gutters, some beside outlines of axeheads or bare feet. I suppose we shall understand them in Heaven, astounded at our earthbound ignorance. The bulk of our examples, in so far as they can be dated at all, pertain to that period of expanding horizons that we label 'The Bronze Age' for our convenience.

The cupmarks remain, and the stones, and the cairns. We still build cairns – horrible cemented things like the black monstrosity at the head of Glen Aray, raised in memory of the poet and novelist Neil Munro, who deserved something better. There are also stone-heaps on peaks and in passes, to which every walker should add a stone for the sake of those who went before. Others mark the footway trodden by old funeral processions, where the coffin was rested on a flat-topped boulder (it must not touch the earth before it reaches the graveside, lest the spirit escape to wander restless and unblessed), and where the stones newly added to the pile told later travellers how many had followed the cortège.

There is yet another kind of cairn. You will find it in a fold of hill-ground where a shepherd lost his way in snow, or at a steep corner where a cart overturned. These are not graves – the dead sleep in the kirkyards – but we lay a stone on them to appease that which here parted suddenly from its clay.

As we come near any of them, even the oldest, plundered or excavated though they be, you may see us hunt about for a pebble to bring in our hand; *cur mi clach air a charn* – I will lay a stone on his cairn, whoever he was, for he was here when I was not, and I am the future of his past.

The Archaic Smile

You there with nothing to say – why are you smiling,
Why do you stare past my shoulder, your great blank eyes gazing
At a peak unattainably far, or a joke that's beguiling,
Or a god like yourself, close behind me, golden and blazing?

Why do you hold your lips parted, and offer no token
To show me your childish beliefs about safety and danger?
Why will you never explain, but leave meaning unspoken
While the hairs of my neck stand up in salute to the stranger?

Only a broken old head carved with primitive cunning –
What's that beside a great modern's profound social thinking?
Only a smile on crude lips – and why am I running
Into the dark, Aphrodite, while you stare unblinking?

Ford, Loch Awe, 1964

3

The Time of Wars

BETWEEN THEM the three heathers spread waves of honey-scented colour over the hills, bell-heather, cross-leaved heath and the true ling together, and in spring our bee-masters move their hives up to sheltered nooks to be ready for their harvest. The third quarter of the year is dominated by the colours of the heather, from the first rosy flush in June to the noontide purple of August and the rusty afterglow of October when the stags roar.

The red deer are themselves a rich rust colour at their mating time, but the rutting stags blacken themselves all over in peat wallows and stand gigantic against the autumn dusk, head up and antlers laid back along their backs, the great chests swollen with air pumped to the lungs in grunting coughs before they let our the weird roar that prickles up one's spine, a sound from the dawn of time.

"Unh...unh...unh-unh-unh-Ahooooo!" dying away in grumbles on the still air; silence rolls back listening, and is pierced again by an answering trumpet-note from the next ridge. The hinds meantime wander around gossiping and looking faintly bored, everlastingly interrupted by the running and herding of their lords, or yielding to the blandishments of some younger lothario who sneaks up while the big fellows chase each other across the mosses.

The noise is tremendous; it bangs about from crag to crag, evoking ancestral memory of wolves howling and the bray of trumpets. Day and night it fills the air and stirs the blood. The pipes and drums of countermarching bands at Highland Gatherings a month before are only an overture to the wild music of *Cervus elaphus* in love, as the Gatherings themselves – betartaned lairds and ladies, returning exiles, visitors laden with cameras, kilted "heavies" snorting and straining at cabers the size of telegraph poles, children prancing through the Sword Dance a-clatter with medals – are only a feeble echo of older assemblies where men mustered for war. Then the Sword Dance was a charm performed on the eve of battle, when to touch the blade with a flying foot spelt death to come for the dancer; then the wrestling was a trial of strength and caber-tossing a rehearsal for spearmen.

Heather is *fraoch* in Gaelic, and *fraoch* means also "fire, fury, passion, hunger". Legend tells of a young hero named Fraoch who swam to a dragon-guarded island to fetch rowan berries for the healing of his love Fionnabhair, the daughter of Maeve. Twice he swam, once he snatched a spray of the blood-red fruit, but Maeve commanded that the whole tree must be dragged ashore; the third swim and the tree's shaking roused the guardian beast. Now Maeve – Medbh to give her name its proper spelling – is the 'Queen Mab' of English folklore and a goddess of ancient Ireland, and Fionnabhair, 'White Shoulder', is a namesake of Guinevere. We are touching the edge of Arthur's world and looking past it to older things.

Rowans are still magical. They grow by garden gates to ward off witchcraft, we never use them for fuel, and their scarlet berries are interwoven through old tales. They drop upon a chessboard to reveal the winning move in a fateful game between hero and giant; or they are love-charms, even elixirs of eternal life. They may be the apples of Avalon, that *Emain Abhlaich* or Apple Orchard where King Arthur sleeps and where the old tales tell of silver bells ringing and white birds singing for the pleasure of spirits awaiting incarnation. Whether – as some Greek and Latin authors thought – the Celtic priests believed in the rebirth of souls, whether like their Brahmin counterparts they taught that men return to expiate sin or enjoy an earthly reward, we can hardly be sure; but the tales speak of two otherworlds – the Orchard and, beyond it in the sunset, the Land of the Young, Tìr nan Òg, from which there is no return. The Celtic Neptune, Manannan mac Lir, was the soul's pilot to Tìr nan Òg; throughout the Celtic West his office was taken over by St Michael, and many are the isles of Michael where spirits gathered for their last journey at All Hallows.

It is all very well to write glibly of 'Celtic Gods'; what has come down to us under the guise of myths and legends is a complex amalgam of many forgotten faiths. The Celts may have worshipped both gods and goddesses, many still faintly identifiable from their names – Tarvos Taranos, the Bull-and-Thunder god, Lugh of the many arts, lord of ravens, Epona the horse goddess – but behind this pantheon we glimpse older shapes that shift and change like the patterns of Celtic metalwork. The very diversity of names conceals, perhaps, a unity of beings; the names are no more than attributes and the deities may be less numerous than the lists of names might suggest. Some may indeed be the gods, and especially the goddesses, of tribes who fell under the power of new masters, as in Irish legends warrior queens vainly opposed the landing of young spearmen.

Be that as it may, the creamy blossoms of the silver-stemmed rowan trees were sacred to the Spring Maiden; the fruit pertained to the Harvest Mother who gave place, when the grey fieldfares flew in to feast on laden branches, to the Old Woman, *a' Chailleach*, the Winter Hag who was goddess also of war.

Autumn was the time for wars. Cattle were fat and ripe for plunder, harvests were safe, and men laid up their sickles and took down the spears. Cattle were wealth, currency and pride to the men of our hills as they were in Aryan India and the Ireland of the *Táin Bó Cuáilgne*. That epic 'Cattle Raid', set afoot by Maeve's envy of a sacred bull, was first set down by Irish monks a thousand years after its composition, but its home is in the world of Homer or of the Rigveda; indeed, these three worlds are closely linked.

A time of barbaric heroism, of kings and chariots and bizarre taboos; a world where gods walk the earth in disguise, a queen's jealousy brings provinces to ruin, lovers escape in the form of swans, beasts speak and severed heads sing – we are on ancient common ground with all such images. To call them 'Celtic', or even 'Indo-European', is simply not good enough; you cannot shovel a whole threshing floor of diverse peoples of widely separate origins into one sack of chaff and label it 'Celtic', any more than you could stuff half the present world's population into a sack marked 'English' because many of them can make shift to understand the works of William Shakespeare in the original.

More than five thousand years ago, somewhere between the Danube and the Volga, a group of cattle-owning tribes evolved a language more flexible and more precise than those of their neighbours. The speech spread as the tribes dispersed east and west, to India, to Asia Minor, through Central Europe to the Baltic shores and across France to Spain. The first people to speak a form of that lilting language in Britain may have been contributors to what we call the Bronze Age; many others followed, chattering in assorted dialects (some said "p" where others said "q", giving *panj, penta* and *pemp* for "five" in Hindi, Greek and Welsh, where Latin and Gaelic use *quinque* and *coig*).

Not all who shared the language shared the ancestry – again, the current status of English suggests a parallel – but words travel with a luggage of ideas, so that such diverse matters as law, religion and counting systems became alike over wide areas of the earth. Traditions of a class structure based on priests, warriors, and free farmers survived in India and in Ireland, at the extreme high water marks of that flooding sea.

Its first waves were most probably formed of bands of young adventurers, outpacing the lumbering herds and laden households, seeking loot, battle, and deeds of daring. The notion accords with both probability and legend. First come a king's seven sons to find their fortune; they slay giants, seize their hoarded treasure, marry their daughters and live happily ever after in magic castles. The giants' subjects are, naturally, delighted to gain gallant young masters; burning huts and screaming women find no place in such joyful narratives.

To those whose homes lay in the path of the advance, it must have seemed rather different. Some groups went under, others moved a few miles and did as they had been done by, others again sat tight and soaked up the newcomers and their whimsies. Some incomers and displaced persons built strongholds, some native groups dug in and stood guard on fortified hilltops.

Argyll is full of forts of every size, from big enclosed crags to tiny rock-stacks where one family might take cover while a raid swept by. The best sites have been used and re-used, enlarged or cut back to fit available manpower, or altered to deal with new weapons. Some could hold a tribe and its cattle, others are impregnable while three persons remain to keep the narrow gate. Many are so cunningly placed that they have served again as militia posts, Home Guard block-houses or Forestry fire-towers. Few have as yet been scientifically excavated, and seldom can one guess who began their building.

High above the mouth of West Loch Tarbert, on its Kintyre shore, rises the bald-headed hill called Dunskeig. (Here one should say that *dùn* stands for any sort of heap or hump, from a molehill upwards). Dunskeig is girdled by a contour-wall, more noticeable now from the Islay ferry than on the ground. This is the oldest fort. At its southward end it is overlaid by an oval wall which has been subjected to a fire fierce enough to melt its stones. At the northern end, by contrast, a little round stronghold has been built, using some of the slagged stones from its predecessors.

It used to be thought that vitrified forts, like that on the south edge of Dunskeig, had been burned deliberately to strengthen them. When one sees how the walls have collapsed into contorted glassy lumps that fall away in slabs and sheets, it seems unbelievable that anyone should imagine such havoc strengthening his building, or should choose to repeat the experiment. No, these are monuments to disaster; fire-arrows or hurled brands have kindled the thatched huts within, timbers spread the blaze to stored grain and peaty wall-cores. Doorposts and spearshafts and mead vats have roared up until those who ran in for safety ran out into the enemy's arms. What mercy they find there one does not care to guess – such mercy as Hecuba found when Troy burned, maybe. Of one thing one can almost be sure – those bold boys with the golden collars, those swordsmen of a hundred herds, were not disposed to hump stones nor their women to grind corn – the cold iron of slavery touched the people of the cairns, the Little People who greatly fear the iron.

But all was not quite lost. The conquered outnumbered their conquerors and by degrees regained some part of their former possessions. The craftsmen, swordsmiths and makers of ornaments, found favour among the first, their masters' custom allowing them the same liberty accorded to poets. As the *Aes Dana*, Men of Skills, they were free to cross tribal boundaries, out of the little closed circles of kinship under some warlord whose singers called him a king. The elaborate structure of that society allowed such an escape for three groups; the poet, the craftsman and the young war-man – the three who might otherwise have split it asunder.

Poets stood on the lowest rung of the priesthood, their lives sufficiently sacred to pass unharmed between embattled armies; their work was to sing of high ideals and great events, splendid weapons and deathless deeds; it is with a sense of anticlimax that we survey the tumbled walls of some *dùn* and realise that here, in this bleak, windswept, cramped cattle-pound, the mighty myths were sung.

Those myths survive only in the faintest echoes, all meaning lost, their outer shells turned into comic tales. They stir in our deepest subconscious like fish in a pool, the last link in a chain of oral learning. There is the Boar Hunt, the ritual pursuit of the fearless beast with the moon-crescent tusks, whose killing was a test of manhood; I have met a man whose father used to take him to "walk the track of the boar" from place to place along West Loch Tarbert, with a part of the story for each stage of the hunt. There are the ravens, who guarded (and still guard) the head of Bran the Blessed on Tower Hill. A young forester told me how he and his mates saw a raven land near them and croak three times. He and two others decided to knock off early; the fourth laughed and carried on alone. When they stopped the van at his house next morning they could not rouse him; going in, they found him dead. He told his tale with all the repetitive phrases, the 'runs' that link ancient stories; and he went on to describe an old stalker's funeral and how a hind came to stand above the graveyard. When the coffin was earthed she turned back to the hill, her farewell said to the man who had loved the deer.

Such things might well have been recounted by the feast hearth in the forts. Within these drystone walls warriors strutted, their hideous trophies of skulls around them, and women unbound their hair to work dark arts. Above them croaked the ravens who know the place of battle and the eagles who know its time; about them spread a web of custom to shield them from the powers beyond.

Enter these enchanted woods, ye who dare – with their arts, poets and craftsmen learned ways to protect themselves from things more perilous than war. The poetry of the bards, as we glimpse it in fragments, was highly formalised and closely wrought; so too was the metalwork of the bronzesmiths. Theirs is a curious, a highly abstract art overlying great technical skill – an art of spiralling designs, cast or engraved or both, with few naturalistic forms but instead masks that break into tendrils, leaves that suggest a face, a flower that might be an eye. It matches the complexity of the poets' tales, illustrating a myth-world where all is implied and nothing expressed, shape melts into shape and thought into thought, all things linked and interacting. Carried across Europe by as tough a collection of barbarians as the world has known, in Ireland it reached new heights of beauty and craftsmanship; when the world that reared it was dead, it flowered on in Christian stonework and the painted pages of gospel-books.

The third group free of tribal bonds were the young fighting men.

They could bind themselves into fraternities, severing family ties and setting off to find a king to reward their daring. They had their own rules, their ferocious initiations, their chosen leaders. The surviving stories of their deeds may be immensely old, may even hark back to those kingly giant-killers; most of the stories now cluster around a band calling themselves the Fianna or *Féinn*, followers of Fionn macCumhaill ('Fingal' in later paraphrases). *Féinn* comes from a word meaning 'warrior, giant, hero', possibly also linked to *féin*, 'self' or 'selfishness'. If that could be proved it might illustrate society's attitude to the fraternities; they left the community for their own venturesome ways and went to keep, or disturb, the peace of another tribe.

The laws took account of them; they might not serve as a unit with their own people, nor marry nor take up inheritance unless they first discharged themselves. Some bands may well have enlisted in Roman auxiliary units, marching to a centurion's command in the Gaulish *pâtois* of the drill book, turning up at home with strange talk of Dacia or Spain. Others may have watched Agricola's fleet sail by, or a few generations later led a rush across the abandoned Wall. They were the earliest professional soldiers in a country that has bred soldiers ever since; later stories turned them into comic giants and Fionn himself into a kind of Colonel Blimp, when the Gael learned to laugh at his heritage if he wanted to keep its shreds.

But still rowans guard the gate, heather scents the air, stags roar by starlight. The boar's head is Argyll's crest, and a boy in jeans watches a mourning hind and heeds the raven's warning.

4

The Song of Deirdre

STILLNESS.

The loch translucent, steep-sided, bottomless, the snow-water a sheet of green glass without flaw.

The grey-green slopes soaring, steep folds, green dresses falling from knees of giants motionless, their heads veiled at two thousand feet by the level veil of cloud.

The folds of the dress marked by hundreds of rivulets; on their day foaming and plunging with mountain rain or melting snow; today dark streaks, creases in the hillsides.

Black shapes on the lower slopes, crouching, waiting. No, look, not black, glossy green; all green here, holly leaves throwing back faintest glow from cloud veil; on their day bright with jewelled berries, today glossy, hunched, waiting.

Rivermouth dark with stones, no life in grey water; cattle on the fan of grass beyond; a few sheep. A scatter of houses – grey house, white house, smoke rising straight, shimmer and drift to the cloud; shelter trees, gardens dug, first leaves on rose bush, hedge neat, waiting.

Hills dwarfing thin trail of road, thin trails of house-smoke, white boat drawn ashore; no wake on water, only a ring of silver spreading, spreading from where the white-breast gull floats asleep.

Glen Etive. Etive triple-guarded, by the Herdsman of the black rock plaid above it in the mist, watching the road dive under his elbow from Glen Coe; loch edged with faintest track each side, ten miles to the narrows and a glacial sill; six miles more of wider waters and the tidal Falls of Lora to lock the outer door; a fiord within a fiord.

Not a bird sings this still morning; pipits work among the beach-stones, sparrows chirp in gardens, a thrush flies out of a holly bush; far up the glen a cock defies the silence.

Far down the loch, an answer. Too far, too faint, we catch but half of

33

it – "-oo", "-oo". The missing note tantalises the ear that strains for it; then, and it must be that the silver bird is rounding some shoulder, some dew bright rowan on the farther shore, we have heard it full and clear. We have heard it, and now the silence has gone and instead a voice is in the air, as clear as glass, as fresh as green, as bodiless as Echo.

> From the hillside
> Calls the cuckoo
> And methinks I hear it still
>
> O Glen Etive
> O Glen Etive
> Where I built my earliest bower...

The haunting music fades, silence again, a breath of heartbreak has passed by.

Where did you build that bower of fiddle-curled royal-ferns? Down near Dail, where the slopes are kinder to three brothers climbing to the hunt? You could have been safe anywhere along the locked fiord, safe from king's lust and king's revenge in your hut remote from guarded courts, you white-handed girl of the doomed beauty, you Deirdre of the Sorrows, with Naise your lover and his loyal brothers who foresaw the evil to come.

You could have been safe, but you went from here, down to Glendaruel where the cuckoo calls in the woods. Fergus will find you there and promise to protect you if you come home with him to Ulster. He is caught too in the net of fate; a trick draws him away from you; his own son and a son of King Conchubar bring you to court in his stead.

They will lodge you in the Hall of the Red Branch where the brothers pass the time with some kind of courtly chess-game and you watch the fire – so strange, a log-fire on iron firedogs instead of the starlit hearthstone and the heather couches. The King's spies peer through chinks; is Deirdre still the fairest among women? One of them lies, trying to save you; no, how could a girl return from the wild hills of Alba as beautiful as before? Ardan looks up, sensing watchful eyes, and hurls a pawn to blind the second spy, the truth-teller.

Armed men come to the door. Fergus's son, Illaun the Fair, dies on the threshold to keep his father's word of safety, flinging his sword to Ardan from a dying hand. Cormac the King's son sets his back to the broken planks for the honour of his own pledged word.

You brothers, you three Sons of Uisneach, this is your place to die. Deirdre will step through your blood to face the King who has owned her from birth, and to plead with the grave-diggers to make a wide grave, a grave where four may lie.

The end is dark. All Gaeldom knows the tale thus far, but many are the turns that end it. She casts herself into that wide grave; not so, they hold her back and drag her away to live a year unsmiling, only raising her head from her knee to sing her song of remembered joy, until the chance comes to throw herself from the killer's chariot; or else – and only once have I heard this – she steals to the grey sea-strand under the moon and there between the tidemarks a grey flint knife sets her free.

She is one with Helen, and Sita, and Iseult the Fair, born to beauty and to be causes of strife. Her story is one of the satellite tales of the Cattle Raid (he always tells it well, but it's too sad – I'll drop in tomorrow night and hear the next part instead. So might a listener prefer *The Catalogue of the Ships* to *The Death of Hector*). Her song has been sung, rewritten, prettied up, harmonised, elaborated for choral competition – it rends the heart still.

Glen Etive in April, glass-green and mist-veiled, waits for Deirdre who will not return.

5

The Centre

THE GREY marsh is three miles wide, reclaimed in part, elsewhere a quaking salt bog barely above tidemark. A few low hillocks break it; above them the grey geese wheel and curlews cry. In summer rare plants flower, and salmon crowd upstream, but in winter the Big Moss is desolate.

A' Mhòine Mhór – the name has the sough of winds in it. Veils of sleet drive over withered grasses and hang in cold walls of glass around the highest rock. It rises less than two hundred feet from the swamp, the first enclosed fields at its feet, but in its setting it crouches like a lion.

A causeway leads to it through the winter-sodden fields, a pot-holed farmtrack down which have gone the feet of spearmen, riding ponies, pack horses and royal chariots, for it was once the highway to a capital.

A steep path climbs to a rock cleft a hundred feet above the plain. Here, within a massive girdling wall, is a green level, and a well whose spring now supplies the farm below. A grass-grown stairway leads to higher terraces, the topmost still showing part of a curved citadel wall and below it to the northward a bare sheet of rock.

There are six things to see on that rock (now given a virtually invisible protective cover). There is a deep basin; a faint barefoot print; a Victorian vandal's scrawl possibly masking an older design; the clearcut outline of a wild boar, and a hollowed footprint pointing to the distant peak of Cruachan; lastly, two lines of Ogam writing. The basin and barefoot print may be prehistoric; the boar and the shod footprint probably belong with the Ogam to the years between 400 and 800 AD, the time of Dunadd's glory. The writing should, in all reason, explain the rest, but it reveals nothing.

Ogam is a simple script. Invented in Ireland, it consists of four sets of notches along a baseline, five each to right and left, straight across or diagonal. It is most often seen on memorial stones, *X son of Y* or the like; The long Dunadd inscription promises something more informative but yields only a string of unpronounceable letters. Once, as I watched one of the greatest living authorities kneeling beside it baffled, I heard the echo of a ghostly chuckle from the bare rock-boss behind me, a rock that forms no part of the defences but might have served other purposes – sacrifice perhaps, or divination, or the composition of cryptic epigraphs.

From the citadel one looks seaward over the marsh and the linked channels of the Add. Where the crag runs out in smooth whalebacks on the southward, local tradition claims that ships once berthed – little ships, poling or towing up river. Among the mass of finds from repeated excavations are sherds of Samian ware and bits of Gaulish wine jars. Adomnan, in his *Life of St Columba*, mentions French wine ships visiting *caput regionis*, "the headplace of the region", and bringing news; maybe these rocks felt the pull of their hawsers.

Look upriver, past the standing and the fallen stones of Bronze Age mystery, and you face the green levels where Kilmichael Tryst was held, the biggest cattle market in the West until the railway reached Oban. We know the market moved there from Kilneuair on Loch Aweside in the 1400s, with the parish church; but perhaps the Tryst was returning to an ancient site, a Fair held under Dunadd's protection like the prehistoric fairs in Ireland, Carman or Tailtiu, linked to the Irish kingships.

The crag in its marsh had long been a refuge, like the crag of Dunbarton where Welsh-speaking British kings reigned; the Dunadd excavations have produced objects spanning several thousand years, though the one thing to which legend testifies is not among them. Once there was a stone, over which St Patrick prophesied and which later Christian legend made 'Jacob's Pillow'. On it the earliest Christian kings in the British Isles were enthroned, the stone being carried forward as their realm enlarged until it reached Scone near Perth. From thence it, or a substitute, was purloined by Edward I of England, under the impression that ownership of the Stone conferred mastery of Scotland. What St Patrick had said was that wherever it rested the race of Fergus should reign – not quite the same thing; his prophecy is still working.

St Patrick was blessing the race of a fifth-century Ulster sub-king. When the Sons of Erc sought their fortunes overseas, their first perilous footholds were on the hems of Alba, around Dunadd, carving each a share

– Loairn to give his name to Lorn, Congall to Cowal, Angus establishing an enduring domain in Islay.

They called Scotland *Alba*, themselves something like *Scotti*, and the new lands *Dalriada* after their Antrim home-ground. Many Irish immigrants had preceded them, they had not to conquer aliens but to establish leadership. Whoever had been in nominal control of Argyll was off to raid the former Roman province, now bereft of legionary defenders, or to help fend off Anglian invasion along the eastern coast, or merely to lift some Strathclyde cattle. Everywhere old alliances had failed, new ones formed, people were adrift – masterless men, former auxiliaries, runaway slaves – all the flotsam of an empire's end.

Roman writers speak of *Angli* and *Saxones*, *Picti*, *Scotti* and *Attacotti*, swarming along the seaboards before the legions finally embarked for Gaul in AD 410. *Scotti* we have met, *Attacotti* might be Galloway men, *Picti* covered all painted or tattooed barbarians, 'fuzzy-wuzzies' to be kept beyond the two Walls or taught a lesson by frontierguards until at last Rome laid down the burden of Empire.

These late-Roman authors are confused and confusing about the Picts – earlier writers ignored them. Perhaps the simplest interpretation of scanty evidence is the best; that there existed, at times and in places, a loose confederation of assorted tribes, from Cape Wrath to the Forth-Clyde line. Some might be pre-Celtic; many used animal totems and perhaps worshipped totemic gods; some spoke Welsh, some Gaelic, others used non-Celtic tongues now lost. Some were survivors of broken tribes, others may have been forcibly transplanted by the armies of occupation. The commentators never got them sorted out.

The little we know about Picts centres on two things – their stonecarvings (and the Dunadd boar is in a Pictish style) and their system of kingship, not unlike the pre-republican Roman system. Kings of the Picts ascended their thrones not in father-to-son succession nor, as the Dalriadic Scots, by election, but through mother-right. Royal sires were often foreigners; royal women did not rule directly, unlike Boudicca of the Iceni, but transmitted power to their sons.

Mother-right – matriliny – and exogamy, marriage outside the tribe, both belong to a primitive social order. They have left us traces; we may still identify a man by his wife's or mother's name ("Katie Campbell's man" is her husband Robert MacDonald, "Katie's Robbie" is her lawful son); in Scots law a woman is cited as "Mrs Campbell or MacDonald". Gaelic proverbs reinforce the custom; "I will not say '*brother*' save to my mother's son". The Pictish tradition produced a succession of rulers who kept Dalriada in its place, by war or alliance, until the balance tilted and a Scots prince gained and kept the Pictish throne for long enough to introduce new ways.

The Dalriadic settlers had imported and modified Irish rules. Back home a dynasty reached extinction when it shrank to heiresses. Irish kings were elected – 'selected' might be better – by spokesmen of their supporters, from a short list of royal kinsmen down to great-grandsons of any former king. This group was the *rig-domna*; its equivalent among lesser men was the *dearbh-fine*, 'true kinship', thirteen adult males of whatever standing, mutually responsible for any one of their families. The relationship was conveniently demonstrable on a hand, the great-grandfather on the palm and each descendant on a different joint.

Only the *rig-domna* provided candidates for the throne; after four king-less generations the branch lost its right, unless some catastrophe wiped out nearer claimants. The title swung between the active branches, each striving to keep its claim alive.

Any blemish, physical or other, disqualified a candidate and might even cause dethronement; doubtless there was a highish accident rate and some skulduggery. Despite that, the system had surprising strength and allowed the tribe to choose the man of the hour – warrior, lawgiver or peacemaker. Traces of it lingered into the Bruce-Balliol dispute in 1291, and showed a last flicker of life in 1689.

The early rituals are lost, but there is a strong presumption that Dunadd's Boar and footprint marked an inauguration place. Elsewhere, primitive ceremonies lasted longer; twelfth-century Irish kings drank a white mare's blood, Lords of the Isles took office standing on a footprint-stone holding the white rod of justice. In 1249 the child Alexander III was enthroned on the Stone of Destiny outside Scone Abbey, among his assembled people. Elizabethan spies reported that a rebel Irish earl had "gone to the Stone to be made".

The Dunadd footprints are so placed that anyone standing in them looks directly to the crests of Cruachan through a notch in lesser hills. The rock basin could hold a ritual drink, the Boar could symbolise courage or be a totem or a mark of Pictish conquest (if so, it seems odd that it was not removed after Liberation; but it has been re-cut, the bristling crest lowered into a meek hog's back, the tusks battered away).

It does seem probable that here the first kings of Dalriada-in-Alba were inaugurated, with lawmen and warriors around them, royal women perhaps secluded in the citadel or perhaps directing the ceremony from up there, the community massed on the lower levels. Fourteen other forts are visible today from Dunadd, probably more showed up before afforestation; they need not have been in use together, but maybe from their walls shields flashed or bonfires streamed in salute. It was sound Celtic custom to fix a kingdom's centre as near as possible to its physical midpoint – no bad thing, as those who are ruled from a distant corner of another country can testify – and to choose a landmark hill or already-revered site (as at Tara). Such considerations would readily dictate the choice of Dunadd.

The king would not live there permanently; his court must move around his realm, if only because it was easier to go where taxes were paid in foodstuffs than to assemble them centrally. There is abundant evidence of permanent workshops, jewellers, armourers and blacksmiths in regular employment.

The Dalriadic kings, like other primitive monarchs, were half divine; on their courage and integrity depended the health of their people and the fruitfulness of the land – but they were not tyrants. They remained subject to law (as indeed the Crown in Scotland is still subject, and can be sued), and the laws were in the hands of highly trained jurists. The *Breitheamhain*, 'Brehons', were of the priestly caste which stood above the warrior caste (from which kings were chosen), and attained their office after strenuous training.

First came seven years of mastering metres and rhyme schemes, and memorising the lays that enshrined tribal history; from that stage they emerged as *Filidhean*, Poets, entering the ranks of the *Aes Dana* with its liberties and secret powers. A poet not only knew his royal genealogies, he could compose a satire which could blast a reputation or strike its victim dead; he could understand the language of birds and beasts, and he stood on the boundary of magic, the darkness beyond the safe world.

Another seven-year course made the Brehon, his memory stored with ancient law. It could only be stored thus, for a deep-laid prohibition banned the reduction to writing of the sacred words. At the other end of the Indo-European world, Brahmins observe the same ban.

There is no point in banning writing unless the means of writing exist. Some Irish stories mention yew wood tablets; perhaps these were used in the schools, and bore Ogam texts – but none has survived. Again, as each Ogam letter bears the name of a tree, one could string leaves or twigs into a message; there is no hint of any such thing. The laws themselves were only preserved, if in fragmentary outline, by the intervention of St Patrick, who caused them to be collected, and endorsed those that did not conflict with Christian ethics. The oldest surviving text is a seventh-century recension of that fifth-century review, and its precision might seem an idealised theory of primitive justice except that parallel practices are found in ninth-century Wales and medieval Scotland. They are distinguished by a single unifying principle – the principle of contract.

No distinction is made between criminal and civil cases. Judgement hinges on a contract kept or broken – between man and man, man and woman, teacher and pupil, master and servant, God and humankind. The principle was acceptable to Patrick and his converts; one biblical commentary glosses Adam's sin as breach of contract – the fruit of the Tree of Knowledge had been expressly reserved in the lease of the Garden of Eden, and "the whole world died for one red apple".

Though bygone cases may be cited, each cause turns upon determination of the contract involved and the extent of its breach. There is no muddle over intention and commission; murder is murder though the intended victim survives. He who aids a criminal – who is "art and part" in modern Scots terminology – is guilty in proportion to the help he gave, and is to be judged with, but after, his principal.

The overriding need was to prevent private vengeance and avert the blood feud. Every fault was healed by compensation, reckoned in cattle, assessed on a scale fixed by status and weighted for skills. Thus a chief who wounds a craftsman pays an amount set by his own position (he should know better) and by the effect of the injury on the workman's ability to ply his trade. The penalty might be laid upon an offender's kinsmen in set shares and distributed among a victim's *dearbh-fine* in like proportions; giving every incentive to collar one's drunken cousin before he got into a fight. Failure to pay was backed by the single sanction of outlawry. There was no more terrible fate than to be expelled from the group, to seek refuge among strangers or lurk like a wolf in the wilderness. *Cha dhuine, duine 'na aonar* – Man alone is no man, a hermit crab without a shell.

Lastly, beyond the Poet and the Brehon, lay the final course that led to the priesthood; here secrecy becomes impenetrable. We know there were priests; Greek and Roman authors called them Druids, and hinted at divination, human sacrifice, weird ceremonials around oak trees deep in northern forests. Later Irish tales, filtered through Christian fingers, present the image of elderly and incompetent magicians, sulking and fuming as some missionary outwits them. What they really did and were remains a mystery. The towering edifice of legend that wreathes Bronze Age monoliths with mistletoe and sets old persons circling them in nightshirts is simply brewed out of stray notes by foreign reporters, eked out with a great deal of vivid imagination in recent times. It is conceivable that some Celtic tribes adopted local customs in their new colonies, while the Bronze Age reached its stormy end, or that some old rituals persisted; but that is the nearest possible link between a standing stone of 2,000 BC and a priest of the fourth century AD.

Probably the priesthood was already losing ground when the new faith came to challenge it; some of them may have relied on elaborate and awesome rituals to keep their flock in order, others may have taken off into ivory towers of abstract thought (the Greeks had already equated Druids with Pythagoreans). Maybe amid tribal wars, flights across the sea between Antrim and Argyll, mounting breakdown wherever Rome had once kept order, the ordinary people turned back to older ways and laid gifts at trees and springs where kindly godlings lived, or consulted the local Wise Woman for commonsense advice. Certainly there was no organised and unified priesthood to withstand any new ideas; many 'Druids' actually joined the missionaries and brought their learning with them. St Columba trained as a Poet, St Kenneth as a Priest (though he failed to qualify).

The fifth and sixth centuries are full of tumult, the sounds of war, the sounds of running feet. Men with spears, men with the last of their household goods or with sacks of loot, men with belated offerings to angry gods, fill the mists; somewhere a woman shrieks, a child sobs. The Irish law texts name "three periods when the world dies; the period of a plague, the period of general war, the period of dissolution of contracts". Cold winds blow, the earth has turned to iron, the scheme of things has fallen apart.

And up through the cracks, like aconites through frozen ground, come points of light. It is time to look southward from Dunadd towards the low brown woods thrusting across the Moss from Barrnakill. The name means 'Bluff of the *cella*, sanctuary or cell or holy grave'; hidden under the scrubwood is a small cross cut into a rocksheet. Nearby in a clearing within a little wall stood a stone with another cross and a few letters in a script that is not Ogam.

Learned among the learned, exiles among exiles, the saints of Ireland are raising their sails to steer towards Alba.

6

The Island Soldiers

ON MAY mornings the islands gleam like jewels on blue silk, from amethyst Islay to emerald Lismore, set in their fringe of islets like the coral or amber studs of Celtic metalwork and beaded with skerries where cormorants dry their wings and the seals haul out to sing. This is the weather that brings back cuckoo and whitethroat, the season when cattle and sheep are landed to graze the lush grasses around ruined walls.

In the long days of summer all islands beckon; we remember the sweet water in the watercress-choked wells, and we long to sail out to the untrodden beaches. But even at midsummer a three-day gale can rise, keeping lobstermen ashore and smashing their creels on the black reefs. The summer visitors think us lazy and unenterprising to leave the islets empty, but in the same breath they ask if we really stay here all winter, and how do we fill the long evenings? If they could see the coasts as we see them in October or February, the striding winds hurling spindrift far inland and the waves piling the wrack on the flayed turf, they might understand that only strong – or desperate – men would choose to overwinter on an out-isle. When the barometer plummets and the air grows heavy and menacing, and a drift of weary gulls drops to inland fields, then we go out and rope down anything that must stay outside, and take in anything that can be moved, and keep a wary eye on the torn clouds beginning to move faster overhead.

Once, driving down Kintyre, stopping every third mile to scrape snow and frozen foam off the windscreen, luffing up for field gates, changing gear to push downhill, I reached the welcome lee of Campbeltown streets to find Davaar Island blocked out by whirling spume and – most ominous of all – the lifeboat's berth empty.

Campbeltown lifeboat lies afloat in the harbour, ready for action. That night she was somewhere between Ailsa and the Heads of Ayr, while on the sheer cliffs of the Mull of Kintyre a rocket crew clambered above a coaster shouldering into the rocks. The Islay boat could not help, for she was away beyond Rudh'a'Mhail in support of the Barra boat breasting the crazed Atlantic surges. On such a night there were many lying awake with a light in a seaward window, in case some lost man had sore need of even so small a gleam.

At all seasons the sea's voice is heard in the gulf between Jura and Scarba. Here coils Corryvreckan, the whirlpool surpassed only by Maelström and Saltström. Half over from Crinan its currents lay hold of a ship's keel, with each tide-turn its growl rises to a roar. In one of its deep caves a Prince of Norway sleeps, with his great hound to guard him; in its cauldron the Cailleach tramps her blankets and spreads them on the hills when the first snows come.

The rushing and roaring, the coils and overfalls, are caused by tides that turn earlier outside Jura than within the narrow Sound. Deer swim across and local boats slip safely through, running on a green shoulder whose crest curves above the gunwale and whose trough is a hull's depth below; but it is no place for ignorance or carelessness. As the tide sweeps westward the little storm petrels dance up the swells and puffins bustle past with parrot beaks fringed with fish; ahead rise the blue Mull cliffs and the jagged crests of the Garvellachs.

Garbh Eileach, the rough rocky place, is a chain of small islands. The northernmost, Dun Chonnaill, is crowned by castle walls; then comes a larger island with deserted houses, a tiny triangle called *Cuile Bhrennein*, Brendan's Nook, and lastly *Eileach an Naoimh*, the Rock of the Saints. Here St Brendan the Voyager, the Kerryman who founded Clonfert, founded also a little community within reach of his friend Columba's Iona before sailing away in his hide-and-wicker curach to Iceland and beyond. There is still a thick-walled chapel, lit by a single eastern slit, an underground well and store, a cornkiln and a herb garden and later gravestones, from the days when Iona took charge; an isolated early grave (traditionally, that of St Columba's mother) and, near the landing place, a clutch of corbelled huts. They might have been built before or long after St Brendan; once they were sheathed in turf to keep them weathertight when the great winds blew. Now they are open to the sky, homes for wrens and pipits, with stonecrop cushioning their stones. From the Skelligs of the Kerry coast to lonely North Rona, these were the homes of the early monastic movement as it spread out

45

from Ireland – not summer retreats, but places where their builders intended to pass their entire lives.

It can be hard today to interpret the pressures that drove people to such solitudes; their normal life was scarcely luxurious; it offered challenge enough without seeking more. Yet the movement had its own stern logic, driven by forces we forget. There was the nature of Celtic society, based on groups, *dearbh-fine* within the tribe, *Féinn* and *Aes Dana* outside it. There was the educational system that produced poets, lawmen, priests, which required some sort of 'college' for the long years of study. There was the tradition of oral learning with its close teacher-pupil relationship. Each of these elements would of itself steer Christian converts towards forming new social clusters; as the bringers of the faith were themselves Celts, naturally they worked within existing patterns.

Christianity reached Ireland during the Roman occupation of south Britain, spread perhaps by refugees from official persecution (it was not adopted as the state religion until after the evacuation of the Province, though tolerated earlier). Third-century North African writers reported rumours that the faith had outflown the Eagles into the uttermost west; before St Patrick, there were isolated groups of believers. The great explosion in the fourth century seems mainly due to gains among the learned classes and some ruling families. Kings themselves might not be able to convert, having ritual duties to perform, but could grant a derelict fort or a minor island to missionaries. Many learned men opposed the new ideas with outraged jealousy, but to others the notion of a sacred book presented a deep challenge. *Sacred learning* and *written record* were sharply contrasting images.

Scholars found a whole new world, a teaching based, like their own, on clear cut principles but enshrined, unlike theirs, on sheets of parchment. The abiding respect throughout Gaeldom for the written word may stem from that early confrontation. First a new language must be learnt, then its alphabet mastered, then they could begin to analyse and debate. Before long they were adding commentaries in Irish, and eventually preserving their own ancient heritage. It was entirely natural that they set up study centres; but yet another necessity confronted them.

All faiths produce their solitaries and their mystics, but a peculiarly Celtic need drove men into the wilderness. In their close-knit society, man alone was no man. Even those who left the tribe did so for some other comradely fellowship. Christianity deals with individuals rather than with groups; the convert must find his own identity, must smelt from the ore of the tribe and forge from the metal of the *dearbh-fine* that curious new product, a personal soul.

Such breaks with age-old tradition are not easily made. Some who had heard of the Desert Fathers went off alone and "with long circuitous voyaging through windy seas" (as Adomnan says) sought private desert places; others adhered to tradition and formed clusters, each man building his stone or wattle hut around a communal kitchen and guest house, with a scatter of tiny oratories to house the Book and admit of solitary worship. There they set out to become a new *Féinn* – they called themselves God's soldiery – and there they read and copied holy texts under the guidance of someone who had mastered the new learning.

As the movement gathered momentum the small communes were overwhelmed by sheer numbers; some grew into veritable university towns whose students needed farms to feed them, craftsmen to prepare ink and parchment and goose-quills, carpenters, masons, smiths. By the end of the fifth century these self styled 'hives of learning' were sending out swarms of mission preachers and revitalising ancient skills. Poets composed hymns; bronze workers made book covers and relic shrines, and helped design the interlaced patterns for gospel books and stone carvings; and still the call to solitude drove the teachers away to some rocky island or hilltop.

It might be useful to make a rough list of dates. St Ninian, a Romano-Briton, who may have had personal contact with the pioneer of Western monasticism St Martin of Tours (d.397 AD), directed his mission to the Picts from his base at Whithorn in Galloway, and died in 432. St Patrick, born about 385, was carried captive from Clydebank to Ireland as a child, escaped, and returned as a missionary in 432, dying about 461. St Brigid ('Bride'), to whom many Argyll churches are dedicated, died Abbess of Kildare around 523; her *Vita* has embraced traditions of her namesake Brigitta, 'Fiery Arrow' and Spring goddess. St Brendan of Clonfert and Garbh Eileach died in 578. St Columba, kinsman of the O'Neill kings but just outside their *rig-domna*, was born in Donegal in 521, began his mission to Scotland in 563 and died on Iona in June 597, just as St Augustine was beginning his preaching to the South Saxons in Kent. St Lugaidh, usually called Moluag, 'my wee Lug', founded his community in Lismore near Oban just before Iona and died in 592. The many places named Kilmory honour St Maelrubha of Applecross (642-722), a major leader in the century after Columba (only research reveals which churches were later renamed *Cille-Moire* in honour of the Virgin Mary; in early times the placenames recalled a missionary or his tutor, rather than Gospel figures).

Kilbrennan, Kilmoluaig, Kilcolmkill, are widespread; even more numerous are 'cells' whose patron is forgotten – Barnakill, the bluff of the *cella*, Achnacille where a grassy ring holds a grave or so, Achnacroish where once a cross stood. Chance may sometimes show how deeply folk-memory has interwoven traditions of many periods.

The northern headland of Loch Sween, in Knapdale, encloses a wide bay. On a green slope stands a medieval chapel, now glass-roofed to protect carved stones gathered from around it, ranging from a ninth-century cross, formerly exposed to storms on the hillside, to late medieval and newer stones; at the east gable excavations uncovered older foundations and rock-cut tombs. The name Keills tells us that here was one of the early teaching places, with a cluster of huts, *cenaculae*. Here St Abban of the family of Cormac taught, and offshore in the tiderace he sought his *diseart*, his 'desert', on *Eilean Mór mhic úi Charmaig*.

The Big Island was too big. Earnest pupils pursued him, built a church (encased in medieval masonry by a pious Lord of the Isles), and encamped about it. An early cross-shaft may mark the founder's burial; a later on the island's crest, was erected by '*Mariota de Ros, Domina Insularum*', (Margaret of Ross, Table 5), widow of the builder. To the south a drystone wall covers the entrance to a rock-slit where St Abban prayed alone, his sanctity so permeating the spot as to confer celibacy on all later intruders. And on this island, tradition declares triumphantly, occurred a miracle that might have scandalised the good man and his disciples.

The Irish hagiographies list two Saints Abban, a century apart. That suited the myth-makers; in his old age, they said, the dear man lived on his island with only his little grand-daughter (how's that again?), until the day he fell into the tide while fishing. The child remained alone till, gathering driftwood, she gathered a bone as well. It sparked and burned her, and nine months later St Abban was reborn.

It seems more like the little we know of Druidism; the idea may go back even further. The theory is of three entities, body, soul and life-force, going their own ways at death, with the 'life' lurking in blood or bone on the lookout for a new harbour free of the bossy soul. This is why we cairn a place of violent death, why virgins must not touch the dead (inducing a nineteenth-century prejudice against girls entering the nursing profession), why only a woman past childbearing may sweep a deathroom and water that has washed a corpse must be poured over an earthfast stone.

That such notions could be linked to a saint's life shows how gently the preachers dealt with their converts. There was no wholesale exclusion of the past; as with St Patrick's appraisal of older laws, whatever was not actually harmful could continue.

Something of the same continuity shows in works of art. In the painted books, and on the stones, coiling tendrils and cryptic masks find a new strength and mingle with designs taken from nature. The artists were not good at human figures, but the bird that perches on a capital, the cat curled at its base, are drawn from life; hymns and chance couplets in a margin are full of the writers' love of nature. The saints' lives are full of animal stories – wolves guard a student's flock, a fly settles down to mark a reader's place in a manuscript – and an old white horse tucks his nose into Columba's breast and weeps in foreknowledge of his death.

This last we owe to our first Argyll biography, the *Life of Columba* written a century after the saint's death by Adomnan, Abbot of Iona. It has its share of miracle and prophecy, its triumphs over hostile druids and over the Loch Ness Monster ('Put that disciple down, Sir! Bad Monster'), but it also gives us the man himself, hot-tempered, energetic, inspiring. Here he joins an embassy to Ireland; there he wades into the sea to curse the pirate who robbed a poor farmer (and who speedily gurgles out of sight). Here, in his youth, he prays when the boat hits rough water off Rathlin, and is abruptly told to shut up and bail; on the same reach of sea, in old age, he tucks up his gown and reaches for the bailer, and is implored to sit still and pray. His absent-minded friend St Kenneth leaves his pastoral staff on Iona (no wonder the man dropped out of druidic school, he had no memory) but Columba forwards it by the power of prayer so that it stands on the Tiree shore awaiting its owner. Again, as he writes in his hut (we can see his handwriting in a psalter in the Royal Irish Academy), he sends his thought to welcome his brethren back from harvest work in the western Iona fields, with "a fragrant smell as of all flowers combined into one".

"An inspired joyousness of heart, strange and incomparable" is Adomnan's description; but still, behind that joy, remained the pain of exile. They recognised three sorts of martyrdom; the green – leaving home in pursuit of learning; the white-exile to spread the word; – and the red. There were few red martyrs in the early years, but many of the other sorts, and they kept a special welcome for any who came to them from home.

Columba sent a young monk to watch for a storm-driven migrant bird, a crane "from the sweet district of our fathers". The boy carried it to the guest house and nursed it back to strength, until "having been a guest for three days, it first rose from the ground and flew to a height; and then, after studying the way for a while in the air, crossed the expanse of ocean and in calm weather took its way back to Ireland, in a straight line of flight".

There were hearts left behind on the green island that ached to follow it.

Levavi oculos

"I have been in the hills all day;
"I have not heard the news".
No, but you heard instead
The mountain mosses singing at your tread,
And saw the views
Heart-lifting, of the shadows in the bay.

      Down, down and down below
      You looked to where men count the days;
      But here, where winter stays
      And sudden drops his cloak and turns to spring,
      Is no such thing.

Here is the open heaven, spinning and standing fast,
Held on the big tops' shoulders; here is height
Soaring beyond mortality; and air
That moves eternal there
Which but to taste, teaches delight
And heals time past.

      And here the spring-foot doe
      Treading across the moss comes curiously,
      Here the white hare sits watching from a ledge
      And there, the very edge
      Of magic, whistling liquidly,
      The golden, golden plover wheel and go.

And hark! What others come?
Wild swans, the soul of storm,
Beating their great vans in the sky
And from long golden throats
Sounding out haunting notes,
The trumpets of an older chivalry;
And, tilting in the wind, the eagles
Not of Rome.

But to come down again,
To leave the holy ground and tread the earth,
In from the brightness of infinity,
Casting the lost glow of divinity
Back to distress and dearth;
Cramping beneath the burdens –
God, the pain!

Cry, for we left our Paradise today;
But when we turn and load
Accustomed burdens, grieving, if we say
"None knows what we forego!"
Then One says, low,

    "I, too, joyfully trod my hills and came away,
    "And bore a Burden up a stony road".

Cnoc an Imheir, Kilberry, 1949

7

Ploughmen of the Blue Fields

KILMUN ON a November morning; the churchtower looming through trees. Memory shapes silvery wraiths in the Holy Loch, a high hull dwarfing submarines alongside, a tender wearing the Stars and Stripes – and farther out, longer ago, legions of every size from *Rodney* and *Queen Mary* to salt-stained corvettes in pink-and-blue Arctic livery, packing the Tail o' the Bank, every gap an anxiety without time to feel it. The road curls inland, across two rivers linking through pastures where snug farmsteads nestle in orchards – a far cry from cold seas.

All changes again past the Colintraive turning. Here larch-needles lie in golden hems along black asphalt, gullies through the plantings grow heather and blaeberries, rust-red bracken, and birches glittering with dew-silvered cobwebs.

In a mile or so the road leaves the firwoods. Here the farms stand apart, each on a green fan where a steep stream rushes to the hill foot. The broad glen is marshy below, boulder-strewn above; brought here blindfold I'd guess myself in Mull, not Cowal.

Past a T-shaped reservoir, the road dives into beechwoods red as Irish gold and sweeps around Loch Striven-head. Over a bare shoulder are more beeches, brilliant in a shaft of sunlight, another loch-head and a crossroads.

To the right, Glendaruel hides six miles of fertile ground, a kindly inn and rosy old church and the road to Loch Fyne. Another road soars westwards towards Kilfinan, its top shrouded today in mist; it is a third way that beckons me – to new ground and a different placename.

We have passed Auchenbreck, Stronafian, Glendaruel – all Gaelic, with nouns ahead of descriptive terms – but here stands Ormidale.

It means what it appears to mean – Orm's Valley. So who was he, and how did he get here? Perhaps his parents had settled in Bute; or he was a merchant engaged in the Irish or Spanish trade; or a pirate waylaying ships in the Kyles' current. Maybe he was all these by turn.

He'd bring his ship upriver on a high autumn tide and lay her up in a naust, a hollow dug into the bank, lined and roofed with branches. Come spring he'd pitch and paint and put to sea, leaving some capable white-coifed woman to manage the farmwork. If he'd prospered, she might have a slave or two, but no slave would ever row in his ship. His cook might possibly be a slave, but if he, or any of the human cargo some ships carried, laid hand on an oar-loom in a tight corner, from that moment he was free. The biggest Norse ship was too slight of hull and scant of freeboard to risk resentful crewmen.

Long ago in north-east Scotland, as I walked to work, I saw a white boat taking shape through fog. I supposed she was carrying survivors from some overnight event offshore, and I began to hurry – and then I saw the flag. It was enormous, a ship's ensign or something from a house flagpole, and it floated proudly, dwarfing the sail. A curly-tailed dog stood below it, barking towards land; two men scrambled among boxes to handle the sail; small muffled-up children were tucked into corners, a young woman nursed a baby beside grandmother at the helm. Three days out from near Stavanger they had reached freedom, and would go on to support the fight from Shetland.

I am glad I saw them. It made clear, better than any book, the Norse settlements in Scotland. Eleven hundred years ago the pressures were different – land hunger preceded tyranny – but the outcome was the same.

In the farthest north existence is still hard. The climate was milder once – Bronze Age farmers harvested grain – but it turned wetter and colder, and no crops ripened. A brief improvement enticed settlers back, but by AD 600, starvation threatened. There was fishing in rich seas, seal-hunting, fur-trapping, even walrus ivory – any available surplus went on corn for bread or ale which must be fetched from Trondhjem or beyond. In sturdy little boats the northerners went to market and heard the talk of the quaysides.

Norse custom shared a man's goods equally among his children. The neighbours made equal heaps of gear and invited the sons and daughters to choose. The land was shared too, and the livestock, and shared again until no portion was large enough to feed a household. Then it was time for one son to surrender his land-rights in exchange for the boat, and seek his fortune on the blue road.

Kinsmen or wife probably had shares in any trading venture; there was only one way to amass something for a favourite child or a woman unentitled to a wife's share. Sword-wealth was a man's own, to bestow as he liked; this is why William the Norman declared all England sword-land to reward his followers. Sword-wealth was the young men's dream. Some made their way to Byzantium to join the Imperial Guard, where they might hit the jackpot, like Harald Hardradi, by outliving several masters; when the Emperor died, his Varangians had a day to collect what they fancied from the palace.

For a young married man the sea-road was preferable. They reached Shetland and Orkney before records begin, spreading to Sutherland and Caithness, to islands sighted on fishing-trips, to long western fiords.

They wanted no warfare. A boatload or two worked together, seeking some corner too barren for local comfort though green enough to their eyes, and there settled among Gaelic-speaking neighbours, one more sort of stranger to be absorbed and accepted. All they asked was a safe landing-place, a share in grazings and fishings and space for a long narrow house. And man, but the fellows were clever in the boats!

Some were keen to farm; as soon as their goods were ashore they began bargaining for a heifer and asking where they could plough. Others had a farther voyage planned when they'd roofed the house and moved the wife and bairns into it. Every spring they would plough and sow, paint the boat and be off, returning for harvest and an autumn run to northern markets, trading a mixed cargo for pitch and iron, and having a yarn with old friends.

That was a mistake; the hard men were listening.

The coasting voyages were little more than a revival of the widespread seaborne trade of prehistory – casual, opportunistic, small-scale. But at the end of the eighth century a tidal wave from the north broke over the coasts of Europe. Iona and Lindisfarne went up in flames; terror spread through Ireland, England, France, Spain, even North Africa and Italy. Christendom added a new petition to the litany: *a furore Normannorum, libera nos Domine*.

From the fury of the Northmen – hermits in windswept huts gave thanks for the gales that swept the sea of keels; smoke rose from churches;

women and children hid where they could. There was no organised defence in western waters – Dalriada had formerly maintained fleets, now there were only rival protection-rackets.

Nothing was safe; settlers and natives suffered alike. Some were even less lucky, for there was a thriving slave-trade with Arabic Spain or by a weary road through Russland to the Volga.

Irish chroniclers label the invaders *Dubh Gall* and *Fionn Gall,* black or white strangers, not distinguishing virtue from vice but merely selecting the colour of the plaited beards; or lump them together as *Lochlannaich,* 'Men of the Bays', (or 'Vikings'). To Norwegian stay-at-homes, Vikings were heroes – wild boys, Argonauts – until some began to cut unproductive sea time and work the Norway coast itself. Today a Norwegian paper may report that police are holding five young vikings after a disturbance...

Where were the kings of Dalriada? For generations they had fought land wars, with Strathclyde, with Anglian Northumbria, with Pictland. In the mid-ninth century, with the Viking terror at its height, Kenneth MacAlpin of Dalriada claimed the Pictish throne by mother-right and the sword, and moved his court to the relative calm of inland Perthshire (shortly to suffer Danish inroads from the east coast).

The west was left to its fate. Iona was sacked thrice in ten years. Some relics were taken to Dunkeld, others moved with the main community to a new home in Ireland – among them the unfinished masterpiece now called the Book of Kells. A small band kept a lamp in Iona through repeated onslaughts. Elsewhere, persecution bred religious revival and small fellowships calling themselves God's Servants, *Celi Dé,* worked among the surviving faithful.

Even when the big fleets lay quiet, lone wolves prowled. Some retired to boast of wild deeds; others fell in battle or quarrels over loot, and sleep in the blown sands. Sometimes companions could spare a dinghy to burn over the grave; at Ballinaby in Islay, a woman's bones were strewn among weapons and boat-rivets.

Some raiders settled as chiefs in the Isles, like Ketil Flatnose whose daughter Aud went to Iceland in old age.

Ketil refused to try his luck in 'that fishing place', though many Hebridean Norsemen set off again for it, taking livestock and slave shepherds, so that most modern Icelandic sheepfarming terms are Gaelic.

Similarly, many Gaelic and English seafaring terms are Norse; so are many 'Gaelic' placenames, not only seamark hills but farms and anchorages. Whatever names passing freebooters may use, people hiding ashore are unlikely to know or adopt them. *Dalr, –vagr* and *-ey* don't become *-dail, -aig* and *eilean* for valley, creek and island, until every child uses them by wont.

The seafarers grew rich on raiding and trading; in Norway, late in the ninth century, one man gained overall control by prolonged warfare. To keep his winnings Harald Fairhair needed fleets and men, and demanded taxes to pay them. No Viking was likely to pay to be overawed, so the rate of emigration rose sharply. There were soon two classes of migrant to the West; smallholders with a fishing boat, a little arable and some rough grazing, calling their new home *Eilif's setr*, or the like, which became Ellister. Others, mostly from southern Norway, took no interest in marginal land; they sought a compact property suitable for a gentleman farmer with business interests, and freighted their merchant ships with goods, gear and slaves. They too called their properties by their own names with *bólstathr*, which rubs down to bus or -bost, as in Arnabost in Coll (Arne's 'bustad').

Seaborne trade continued to grow. In Colonsay, Gigha and Knapdale, folding pocket-scales have been found; Iona, Inchkenneth, Islay and even a Kilmartin cairn have yielded hoards of foreign money – mainly Anglo-Saxon but also some Arabic dirhems. There was no international standard, coins were simply bullion, passing from hand to ready hand by weight.

King Harald could not allow all his potential taxpayers to escape. He sent fleets to find them, optimistically appointed local worthies as tax gatherers, honoured some with the title of *jarl* (formerly meaning something like 'shaman', in christianised usage nearer 'earl'). The biggest jarl in every sense was Sigurd the Stout of Orkney, who in 1014 brought his bulk and honours to visit his sister and her husband Jarl Gilli (or Gille-Bride) of Colonsay. The saga says Gilli 'spoke Norse haltingly'; he was not the last Islesman to inhabit two worlds. Sigurd went on to die at Clontarf, helping the Irish-Norse depress native pretensions and failing when Brian Boroimh broke the invaders at the price of his own life.

The Isles were full of half-Gaels; Norse skills were shared, Norse words slipped into use; crosses were carved with runes and coiling beasts or plaitwork. Upon old patterns fell new social organisation and laws.

It may seem surprising that pirates upheld laws with intensity. Aboard ship, crews voted on the next foray; spoils were shared as fishing-boats today divide the week's takings, with the boat's share going for her upkeep. Longships must land the cook daily to provide hot meals, except on long passages; if they needed bailing more than three times a day, the crew could abandon ship. The sea-laws were practical and well-tested, so that Richard the Lionheart – heir of Vikings – revived them as 'the laws of Oleron' (a Viking base near Bordeaux) for his crusading fleets.

Ashore, the wild men showed a passion for litigation, meeting at local law-mounds, *thingvellir*, and sending delegates to larger assemblies. Women owned property and could divorce husbands by declaration at bedside, hearth and at house-door, removing half the household goods down to the web on the loom. *Lagmenn*, speakers of assemblies, were respected citizens.

In other matters the Norsemen blended into the background wherever they settled. They brought home useful novelties, such as small horizontal watermills that freed women from the drudgery of grinding corn in hand querns. They shipped a bull or a stallion or hunting-dogs to improve local stocks, and like seamen everywhere they picked up local speech. I have heard a Norwegian coxswain and a Highland lobsterman abusing each other over priorities at a jetty, in identical cadences.

By now we are high above Ormidale, with sunlight glinting on the tiderips far below as the mists begin to shred. The road plunges to Tighnabruaich, new ground to me, though I have known these waters from babyhood, passing back and forth, every busy little pier a milestone. Nobody in their senses went by road; nobody in Norse times trudged overland except in the gravest necessity.

Once we reach the shore again we are into Lamont country, passing places with Norse names, Ascog and Lindsaig. The Lamonts were part of an Irish eleventh-century colony, welcomed into Knapdale and Cowal by Scots kings as bulwarks against further Norse penetration. MacSweens, MacGilchrists, MacNeills, Livingstones, MacLachlans – all kinsmen of the Northern Úi Néill, High Kings of Ireland; though surely a few drops of Norwegian blood had filtered in. MacLachlan sounds very like 'son of the Lochlannach'; and isn't *Laumon* an Irish form of *Lagmann*?

This is half-Norse country; but it was never Norway.

Across the loch lies Kintyre, truly a province of Norway's empire, divided from Argyll by Tarbert and the bluffs of Knapdale; beyond Knapdale rise the blue peaks of the sea-kings' realm.

Our road bears away to what Neil Munro always called 'real Argyll'; yet the salt is on our lips.

Erik of Greengarth's Song

I built my steed of the roaring pine,
Her oars of the white-ash cold,
And I turned her head to the storming brine
To garner the ocean's gold.
And not for me the golden grain
Or the horses of the land –
With skis of war I'll hunt my gain
From the high-seat-ruler's hand.

> Then swing up the round shields
> And let the swords be seen,
> For I'll plough the blue fields
> And you'll keep the green.

The width of the world is mine to roam,
My steed is broke to the sea,
The winner of gold is by my side,
The bright-edge plough for me!
I'll seek the praise of the giver of rings
In the heart of the shield-wall-flame,
For the sake of a song the singer sings
And the praise of a deathless name!

> So swing up the round shields,
> And let the swords be seen,
> For I'll plough the blue fields
> While you keep the green.

I'll turn again from the swan-field way
And bring you ocean-fire.
I'll stable my horse in a quiet bay
With harvest of heart's desire.
But ever again I'll seek the main
Where the great sea-horses stride –
The cattle of ocean be my gain
With bright-edge by my side!

    Then swing up the round shields
    And let the swords be seen,
    For I'll plough the blue fields,
    And you'll keep the green!

From Young Hugh, *Kilberry 1964*

Note

I wrote this for an adventure story, and was startled to be asked in which saga I had found it. It is a much-simplified imitation of Norse heroic verses, which were embellished to the point of unintelligibility by the use of 'kennings', elaborate synonyms for weapons, ships and men. The last thing the poets wanted was to call a spade a spade; 'skis of war' is a common kenning for ships, 'ocean fire' and 'cattle of ocean' are wealth won overseas, a 'bright edge plough' is a sword, kings are expected to be 'givers of rings'. I suppose half the fun for the hearers was to work out allusions quickly enough to be the first to applaud.

The name Ascog, a Lamont castle, may itself be a 'kenning', since *askr-* means both 'ash tree' and 'oar' (and thence 'ship'); -og is a rubbed down form of *vik* a bay or *vagr* a creek.

We, and the Lamonts, pronounce their name *Lamm*-unt in these parts.

8

The Crossroads

A GREAT ragged, jagged, blue-black mountain crest, a comb to fit the cockerel that crows to wake the world, blocks the south horizon. The blue-silk sea runs to kiss the feet of Goatfell and Cir Mhór. Over the boat's stern lies the green Kerry shore of Cowal; under the arch of the sail, the brown bluffs of Mealdarroch. Haul the sheet a trifle, and lay her head on the lone tree of Barmore; the next tack will fetch the East Loch entrance.

If you didn't know the coast you would think we were beating towards mere barren hills, with a streak of road and patches of woodland below them. The head of Sliabh Gaoil, square-topped whichever side you see, sits remote and distinguished at the core of South Knapdale; a wild place, fit enough to be the "Forest of Love" where Fionn's nephew Diarmaid fled with Fionn's wife Grainne when she bespelled him.

Ready-about – lee-oh; as the boom swings across you sight rooftops, and a church spire. So there is low ground yonder – an inlet, a pier, an ivy shrouded tower, rocky islets and a red beacon, neat villas fringing the shore, a dense reedbed of yacht masts; there's more to this than you could guess from Loch Fyne.

You are in Tarbert. Not Tarbert Harris of the sounding winds, nor Tarbat Ness sheltering Dornoch, nor yet Tarbet Loch Lomond where the fifty longships crossed in 1263, but Tarbert Lochfyne of the 'silver darlings'. The fishing fleet is here to prove it, moored six deep along the Fishquay by the new covered market, with all their orange and blue and green gear stowed and shipshape. In the middle of the harbour is the squat lump called the Bieldin, which used to have a windlass on it to help laden gabbarts clear the quay in the days before auxiliary engines; inshore of the Bieldin lurks the gravelspit where visitors ground their hired dinghies, to the joy of little boys who scull to the rescue when they can stop laughing. Above the quay looms the castle – James IV's tower, Robert I's keep, whose walls before that?

You can almost scent the space beyond the bayhead, almost expect the ground to open and let you sail through to the West Loch a mile away. This is what all Tarberts are, portages and shortcuts between waters. James Watt proposed making his canal here rather than at Crinan, but those long muddy western shallows daunted him (and rightly so).

Tarbert had managed nicely without a canal and continues to do so, When a hurricane blew several fishing boats aground in the West Loch, they were jacked on to lorries and trundled back to be re-launched in the harbour. Faded photographs show fishing cobles being drawn across on sledges, by cart-horses, to avoid the perilous passage between Rathlin and Kintyre to the outer grounds. Tarbert people will tell you that Robert the Bruce took a fleet that way, on his campaign to capture Castle Sween; to hear them tell it, they'd been there themselves and heard the King cursing when a ship slid off the rollers just opposite the Village Hall. They say, too, that some old Viking had done the same, for a dare or a tear (which is our word for a bit of a daftness), or because he pretended Kintyre was an island.

Ach, it's old blethers, yon; and a lot of superior persons have agreed. If they had paused to check some sources, and especially the Norwegian royal saga called the *Heimskringla* of Snorri Sturluson the Icelander, they would have found it a matter of common knowledge – "there longships are often drawn across", says Snorri. Very recently a bed of massive oaken sleepers has been found on the probable route, and some can be seen in the new Heritage Centre, *An Tairbeart*.

As for that legendary 'Viking' – maybe he considered himself one, for the word had not yet lost status – but he was also King of Norway and could juggle the balance of power from North Cape to Fastnet.

His name was Magnus, called after Charlemagne and given the byename *Barfotr*, "Bareleg" or "Barefoot", because he had adopted the kilt during his boyhood in the Isles. He was reared there because, being the son of a king's concubine and that king wedded to a Danish princess, the climate of Norway was unhealthy for him. His father was known as Olaf *Kyrre*, "the Quiet", which was not meant as a compliment, and when Magnus succeeded to the throne his first task was to recover all that the quiet man had let slip.

Magnus had been a Viking from his twelfth year, raiding and trading with his foster-father between the Isles and Ireland. He returned to Norway with a loyal nucleus of ships and men, and soon gathered others who liked his style. In four years he set Norway to rights and could look farther afield.

He began with Orkney, a Norse colony that had broken away to virtual independence under its late earl, Thorfinn Sigurdsson the Mighty. At his death two of his sons had shared the earldom in accordance with Norse custom; the third son was too young to take up his share yet, which was lucky for him – his elder brothers were packed off to a Norwegian prison and died there. They were close kinsmen of Magnus, which availed nothing. Their sister Ingebiorg imported a further complication (here it might be useful to glance at Table 2, p.213).

Ingebiorg had been given in marriage to young Malcolm Duncanson, King of Scots, whom his subjects respectfully called *Ceann Mór* ("Big Head"), and who had returned from refuge in England to revenge his father's death on the usurper King MacBeth. Malcolm and Ingebiorg had three sons, of whom only Duncan reached manhood; Ingebiorg herself died by 1069 and Malcolm married again.

To Scottish indignation he picked another foreigner, this time a half-Saxon, half-Hungarian princess – a connection that threatened to embroil the country in trouble with the new Norman regime in England.

Malcolm has been depicted (mainly thanks to his new queen's adoring biographer) as a northern boor, kneeling to kiss the magic books he could not read, grunting a few words of broken English in his uncouth lovemaking. In sober fact he was as English as Margaret and probably better acquainted with that country, since he had spent seventeen years in exile there, and she had only recently arrived when her reluctant father had been recalled to take his place as Edward the Confessor's heir-apparent. After the Norman invasion of England Margaret's brother and widowed mother displayed a talent amounting to genius for involvement in anti-government plotting, despite receiving generous treatment from the authorities; the family was in flight after one failed rising when they arrived in Scotland. Malcolm was intent on modernising his kingdom, and used Margaret's help to bring in learned Benedictine monks and skilled Saxon bureaucrats; Norman mercenaries had arrived already, but they had died to a man around MacBeth at Lumphanan. The Scots reserved judgement on these changes, but noted that Duncan had been shipped off to become a hostage in William the Conqueror's hands, leaving the new Queen's growing family to thrive at home.

Duncan's turn came at last when Malcolm and his eldest son were killed near Alnwick, invading England in support of the weathercock Edgar Aetheling. The news of their deaths killed Queen Margaret, and Duncan rode north with an escort of Norman cavalry. He was given only some months to enjoy the throne before the Scots rose in support of his uncle Donald *Bàn*, killed King Duncan and sent his small son back into exile. The eldest surviving son of Malcolm and Margaret threw in his lot with Donald *Bàn*.

Donald the Fair knew his country better than Malcolm could. His youth had passed in the Western Isles, and with the Islesmens' help he kept his throne, like the tough old warrior he was, through three years of warfare. The other sons of Margaret got him in the end, in 1097, which happened to be when Magnus had settled Orkney and was moving into his boyhood stamping-grounds.

As soon as he reached the Hebrides he set about deposing any chief reluctant to toe the line; then he passed on to rout a brace of Norman earls in Anglesey and leave his mark on the Norse kingdoms of Man, Dublin, Waterford and Wexford. Already homeward bound when he heard of Donald *Bàn*'s fall, he paused to think about a new prospect. Here *en passant* lay Scotland at his mercy, war-torn, uneasily led by Edgar Malcolmsson who, once again, owed his throne to William Rufus and his mailed men. Why should not Magnus interest himself in his cousin Duncan's brat? Why not set up a grateful puppet king? Why not, indeed, look a bit farther; Norse colonials had lately taken both Sicily and England; a Norse king could surely do as well. England was reported to be restless (two years later an arrow would fly in the New Forest and kill the Red King). Unlike William the Conqueror, Magnus had no need to build invasion fleets; one lay ready at anchor around his flagship.

Orkney, the Isles, Ireland, Scotland, England – one who was man enough to master Norway could weld that lot together. He was not Harald Hardradi's grandson for nothing; he brought his ships into the Clyde.

Edgar's advisers could have no doubts; this was catastrophe. They had long abandoned any pretence of controlling the West, heavily penetrated as it was by Scandinavian settlers. There was no Scottish fleet, no standing army; the irregular levies were sick of fighting, or only too ready to start private wars. The only hope was to copy old Aethelred, down in England, and buy peace.

"Danegeld?" a councillor snorted; "What Danegeld? It never worked; miss one instalment and what have you got? A sea-king on the doorstep. As for the western men, half of them followed Donald *Bàn*, most of them would cheer for Magnus. People back here grumble enough about half-Saxon kings and Norman allies; if news of that fleet leaks out, we'll face a mass onslaught from every side."

Some unsung diplomat led a deputation westward, wondering which hideous death the northern fiends would inflict on him.

He found his sea-king at anchor in a snug harbour, and found him in a friendlier mood than he had feared. Magnus had been sounding out local opinion. For a start, nobody cared a hoot for young William fitzDuncan – one more unknown brat with a foreign name; all anyone wanted was to be left minding their own business. So he received the Scots ambassadors amiably, and proposed a deal. No, not money; he doubted but he had rather more laid by than they could offer. Instead, he would accept a clear title to every western island round which a ship could sail; would they care to discuss that suggestion among themselves?

Yes, o yes, they would indeed, the difficulty was to maintain a diplomatic calm. "What use are such places anyway? Which of us ever set foot on them? Quick, you stand up and say we agree. Look, he's nodding, by the Black Rood of blessed Queen Margaret we have an accord!

"But here, what's this? He's shouting orders; they're hauling one of those damned great ships up the beach ... they're landing shields and weapons ... has that interpreter let us down? Is it war after all?"

Magnus is down by the shore. He watches his men lighten the flagship as she lies on the dark gravel beach, her steering oar cocked up astern like a duck's tail and her walrus hide cables ranged out ahead of her; then he turns to the sweating delegates:

"Now, gentlemen, let's be clear. You give me every island I can round? (Tell those Kintyre fools to be quiet, Ulf, or by St Olaf I'll quieten 'em! Do they think I'm selling them? They're not worth their freight to market – no, don't tell them that). Ja-so, good; now watch."

They have brought down some massive tree trunk rollers, and stepped the mast, and they stand by the halyards. Magnus swings himself aboard and takes post where the tiller would be if they hadn't just unshipped it. The sail unfolds, spreading its black raven; from all the ships, men have mustered along the hawsers; a skald strikes up a hauling chanty.

Way-hey and up she rises, slowly up the first steep pitch, faster through the hollows, rocking along, the gilded windvane flashing, sail-thrust and cable-heave past the midway cairn; downhill now, easy, 'vast hauling, check her with the hawsers abeam and heels digging into the earth alongside the slideway; out across the mud shallows; afloat in the West Loch while men are still wading beside her.

"You'll agree that I passed yonder with the sail drawing and my hand on the helm?"

What can they do but agree? It savours of magic to them, but it's nothing beside some of the passages on the River Road through Russia. Kintyre has been proved to be an island; Kintyre is Norway now.

Five years later Magnus was dead, caught in a flight of Irish arrows out of ambush. He had uprooted rulers and changed the patterns of masters and men, but his quarrelsome sons soon tore his realms apart. For a generation nobody had time to bother about the fringes of empire. Magnus's son Sigurd would indeed sweep past, bound for Jerusalem, but instead of taking the swan's road home he would dedicate his prows in Byzantium and return through Russia to a shared throne and an end in madness. Some of those Magnus had exiled would filter back, Gael and Norseman alike; new alliances would form, new leaders arise. Little by little the sea-king's deeds would slip into legend and fairy story.

But still Kintyre is not 'real Argyll', and the road between the lochs, with its Heritage Centre beside it, marks a frontier.

Fàire m'Oige

Sud e m'fhàire san Earrach is crìochan mo fhradhairc'sa Chéitean,
tràth thilleadh gealghrian a'mhochtrath s a h-uilinn sna cnocain ag éirigh,
cnoc air muin cnuic anns a'Cheathramh, na mullaichean s leac-ainnean éibhinn,
guala s guala bhòidheach, na tomain an Còmhal s na sléibhtean,
uchdach air uchdaich a'domhlachadh, aonach is mòinteach nam féithean.
Seall, Sliabh Gaoil a'sìneadh san ògsholus fhiòndearg ghréine,
rogha is taghadh nan sliabh, beinn-sheilge Dhiarmaid s na Féinne,
druim fada mìn air deagh shneadheadh, mar bhalla a chasgadh na séisde,
a'sruthadh 'na sliosan s ag aonadh 'na ruigheachan faon ris an réidhlean.
An rìgh am meadhon a shluaigh, deagh bhuachaill am meadhon a threudan -
còir gach rìgh sin s a urram 'na àite suidhe is éirigh;
seasadh a mhuinntir deas air is clì air ag amharc s ag éisdeachd -
an cridhe na h-àirde tuath sud Cruachan Beann fo bhreid ghil,
stuadh a'chìrein àirdghil sìor bhriseadh air fàire s leus deth.
B'e sin clachtharruing mo shùla, an casthonn trìcheannach glégheal.

My Youth's Horizon

Yon was my horizon in the Spring and the bounds of my sight in the Maytime, when the white sun of morning would return with its elbow on the knowes arising, hill upon hill in Kerry, the summits and the joyous hillsides, shoulder upon bonny shoulder, the hillocks in Cowal and the high hills; ascent crowding upon ascent, upland and moorland of the bog-runnels.

See Sliabh Gaoil stretched out in the young wine-red light of the sun, pick and choice of all hills, hunting mountain of Diarmaid and the Fiann; a long smooth ridge, finely carved, like a wall to check the siege, streaming down in flanks and joining in gentle slopes with the flatland.

The king in the midst of his people, a good shepherd in the midst of his flocks – that is the right and honour accorded to every king in his place of sitting down and rising up; let his people stand to right and left of him looking and listening – in the heart of the northern airt Cruachan under a white snood, the wave of the high triple crest ever breaking and gleaming on the horizon. That was the lodestone of my eye, the steep, bright wave, triple-crested.

Gaelic and English by George Campbell Hay, from O Na Ceithir Àirdean, *Oliver & Boyd, 1952*

9

Of Caves and Kings

THE LIGHT BREEZE pushes small clouds to trail fleeting rainbows and bring the scent of primroses from rock-clefts. Over the black Morvern cliffs, waterfalls drift like smoke rising from cave-mouths far below.

The moist air rings. Willow-warblers trill, larks soar to air pibroch-themes, pipits parachute down cascades of song. It's time to watch for the first swallow, to munch a crust at daybreak for fear the cuckoo catches us fasting.

The *Sguabag*, the little broom of a squall that cleared winter's cobwebs, has swept stinging past. The Winter Hag made a last attempt to batter down the young grass, flung her wand under a holly where nothing grows, and fled on the wind's back. Now comes the Cuckoo's Greening, *glasadh na cubhaig*, and *Là buidhe Bealltuinne*, the golden day of May – time of awe, no work to be attempted, and the Spring Maiden's bird shouting day and night.

From Kintyre to Ardnamurchan the woods waken. Pussy-willows turn from silver to gold, basket-willows ruffle emerald feathers along crimson rods. Wind-bowed oaks are bronzed, black ash-buds burst, beeches in sheltered corners dangle three-cornered green handkerchiefs. Wild hyacinths open among the rocks, not yet in carpets like blue woodsmoke. It's the time of new beginnings, boat-painting and blanket-washing and dawn-to-dusk patrols alert for a young lamb's cry.

The Blackface sheep brought sorrow into Morvern when Patrick Sellars arrived from Sutherland boasting of his success in replacing humans by profitable flocks. We had been sheepmasters long before the Clearance, with little tan-faced flocks in fives and tens, herded and housed, virtually pets answering to their names, immune from most ills and providing milk and cheese, warm fleeces, and ultimately mutton-hams. Their ancestors arrived with our own farming forebears, and improved through canny breeding and feeding, not least by the skill of Cistercians. Those white-robed, black-cowled monks established an international trade in the Borders, together with Flemish weavers; the brethren who entered Kintyre in the twelfth century were in close touch (no other Order kept such mutual contacts), but came from Mellifont in Ireland to Saddell in east Kintyre.

There the monastery's head-dyke still runs along the north crest of the glen. The Monks' Burn slides chuckling down the south side; trespassing rhododendrons hide stumps of walling; the grass is deep where the refectory stood; over the guest-house rises a classical portico commemorating an eighteenth-century laird.

Parts of the chancel survive, and there the Clan Donald Society has placed a plaque to record that somewhere hereabouts lie the bones of their progenitor, Somerled the Great.

The community was barely established when they had to chant the founder's requiem. Somerled and his son Ragnald ('Reginald') were both monastery-founders, as befitted their status. Somerled had great plans for Iona also, but left Ragnald to fulfil them, bringing learned Benedictines to replace the Columban incumbents (at the cost of armed resistance) and installing his sister Beatrix as first Prioress of a new Augustinian nunnery.

A later MacDonald bard calls Somerled "a well-tempered man, in body shapely, of a fair piercing eye, of middle stature and of quick discernment". His name is Norse, 'Summer-sailor', and he had Norse blood, but the line that fixed his destiny ran back to Angus Mór of Islay around AD 500. (Table 5, p.216).

One man is as far from Adam as the next, and blood-royal no guarantee of easy living. King Magnus Bareleg bundled not a few chiefs out of their islands, among them Gill'-Adamhnain, son of 'Jarl Gilli' in Colonsay. Gill'-Adamhnain's son Gille-Bride crept off to Morvern; nobody thought much of him. He and his boy existed in a shoreline cave, landless and luckless.

Then one day a man came round the headland bearing a charred arrow as a war token. The old wolves were back – remnants of Magnus's fleet, masterless islanders, northern adventurers – and the local MacInnes chief was summoning every able-bodied man to defend the countryside. Old Gille-Bride could only mutter that he had nothing to offer, no sword, no heart for battle; but young Somerled caught up a cudgel and went happily to the rendezvous.

Local Gael and local Norseman gathered against the common foe. Norsemen were not in the habit of being overawed by others' pretensions, and the Gaels' "blind devotion to a chief" is a myth based on a misapprehension. Devotion was not blind; it rested on kinship and trust. The chief was chosen from proven candidates; if he fell short of expectations, there were others who might do better. No reverential theories could keep him in the job. The boy from the cave must have proved himself from the first charge, the first shout of a half-forgotten warcry, before he could lead a guerrilla band.

Beating off raids was good, but not good enough. Legend suggests a triumphant advance from island to island, overwhelming all opposition with flash of swords and ring of trumpets; reality lies nearer the ground, with a helmet to fit a herd-boy, a sword taken from a dead pirate's hand. Somewhere they captured a ship, patched up the rigging and set off to sea, bringing Coll and Tiree whooping in to share the sport, sweeping on from creek to bay – but this is all guesswork; only the end is sure.

Islay had been the heartland of Angus Mór's kingdom. At Finlaggan in Islay there is a loch, and on the loch an island, and on the island a stone and in the stone a footprint. Here Angus Mór had stood; Somerled's gang escorted him to Finlaggan and proclaimed him King of the Isles.

To Irish chroniclers there was already a *Righ Innse-gall*, King of the Isles of the Strangers. The whole island-chain from Man to the Butt of Lewis had long been ruled by a Norse dynasty. Magnus broke it up, but the links were rejoining like spilt mercury. Olaf *Bitling* now reigned in Man. Perhaps he welcomed a strong young sub-king in Islay, a troublesome corner where his grandfather Godred White-hand met his death.

Time passed. Somerled married, begat sons, extended his scope. At last he asked Olaf for a daughter's hand to seal their alliance. Olaf hesitated, or perhaps his daughter Ragnhild knew of too many other ladies already in Islay; legend says that Somerled's men sabotaged Olaf's ship off Ardnamurchan, so that the bridegroom could sweep to the rescue and enforce the bargain.

By then Somerled had a stronger ally. The last of Queen Margaret's sons had reached the Scottish throne after a weary apprenticeship. Nine years old at his parent's death, David had lived through five reigns – after his father, a half-brother, an uncle, and two brothers had preceded him to the Stone of Destiny (Table 3, p.214). As Queen's brother at the English court he ruled Cumbria in a joint dependency between both kingdoms, and held English earldoms in his wife's right. When he returned north aged forty, bringing his household knights, he came as the most experienced administrator alive.

He can have had few illusions. He must establish himself in restless country, restore neglected laws and introduce new ways, found trading-towns, bring foreign monks to spread education and modernise farming. He knew the reckless men of Galloway well; he spoke Gaelic and Flemish, dismounting to talk with chance-met travellers, and Manx ships traded into his Cumbrian harbours. The half-independent Prince of Galloway, Fergus of the Strathclyde-Welsh blood, was Olaf's father-in-law and also akin to Somerled.

Fergus knew exactly what David's arrival meant. He warned Somerled: "The Scots have got themselves a man this time, and don't you imagine otherwise. He'll not bother you unless I lend him ships, but I'll do just that if you start any nonsense. He's hankering after Kintyre – a few new traders will liven Tarbert market, and though he's promising Kintyre revenues to some of his new monasteries the grants are 'from the year I myself receive them', and you and I know he'll be lucky if he sees a single hearth-penny."

Perhaps Somerled made one trial of strength. Early in his reign David was on the Clyde – presumably with Fergus, since there was no Scottish fleet. The fine Romanesque church of St Blane in Bute, built before 1150, may well mark an accord between three potentates. Blane had been a Dalriadic prince, so a church in his name honoured both David and Somerled. Fergus, zealously church-building in support of royal policy, very probably despatched masons for the work.

Peace lasted through David's life (though Argyll men marched under his banner in 1138, when he intervened unsuccessfully in the English troubles between his niece and his other sister's son-in-law). At the end of his long reign he set Somerled a useful example.

Only one of David's sons grew to manhood, and he died a year before his father, leaving three small sons. David sent the eldest, Malcolm, around Scotland to be acclaimed his heir. Since Scots still, in theory, elected their rulers, this was high-handed, but general admiration for the old king overcame resentment.

When David died, Malcolm was peacefully enthroned. Around the same time Olaf of Man was murdered; his son Godred reclaimed the throne but aroused some opposition whose leaders approached Somerled. In response, Somerled sent his eldest son by Ragnhild on a progress through the Isles during 1155. Lewis, farthest limit of the Manx realm, was also the most loyal; a boat slipped past Islay to warn Godred.

Somerled held a great Yule-feast in Islay that winter, around a hundred ships berthed along the coasts. He promised his guests to have young Dugald reared as future king, if they so wished; and he sought their views on another matter. The Scots had accepted a weak-kneed brat in place of old David, God rest him; there might be another candidate. No, not that Anglified grandson of yon poor Duncan that lasted less than a harvest-time – he meant his own kinsman Malcolm mac Aedh, by rights at least King of Moray. He had fought for his rights, and lain in Scots bondage twenty years – now he was free again. Grandson of a King of Scots, nephew of a king in Moray, the north would rise, Galloway was ready – friends, I give you Aedh's son Malcolm, rightful King of Scots!

The cheering drowned the steps of a man running through the hall, snow on his cloak. He brought news; King Godred was on the sea.

The feasting ended; men trudged away to clear snow from decks and rowing-benches, to hone spears and whet swords.

The *Chronicle of Man* is vague about details, recording only that Somerled's ships gathered 'on the north side of Islay'. The only rendezvous big enough for a fleet is Whitefarland Bay on the Jura shore; east of it, a volcanic dyke juts into the sluicing six-knot tide. The rock is *Stac Mhic Amhlaibh*, Olafson's Rock. It was here that Somerled awaited the Manxmen.

They arrived at nightfall on Epiphany, 6 January 1156. Norse sea battles were rarely fought in winter, when ships should be safe in nausts. There were standard tactics – a hail of arrows followed by grappling ship to ship, with anchors thrown across and axe-blades hooked into gunwales. Thus from dusk to dawn they fought in doomed partnerships, drifting under the stars and the flicker of Northern Lights. Dawn showed a carnage so frightful that Godred made instant peace.

It cost him half the Isles. The straggling kingdom had been divided for administration into *Nordureyur* and *Sudreyur*, North and South Isles, the boundary running due west from Ardnamurchan. Now Somerled gained the Sudreys, while from Muck to Lewis delegates sailed past to the Tynwald of Man (where empty seats still await them).

Somerled was well content, but when his Scottish war fizzled out, MacAedh making a deal with his Scots namesake, the old warrior turned back to Man, evicting Godred to rule the whole island realm.

It was a personal kingdom; Godred would venture home when Somerled's sons quarrelled; but for the moment all was quiet.

Once Somerled joined Fergus and others in revolt against Malcolm IV's fondness for alien ways; thereafter he made peace in ceremonies so splendid that charters were dated 'in the year after *dominus Sumerledus* spent Christmas with the lord King'; but the concordat was short-lived; in May 1164 he brought a fleet into the Clyde.

The intention is unclear; before the campaign got under way Somerled was killed near Renfrew by local levies. A clerical commentator reports, with fervour:

Sed in prima belli rima dux funestus cecidit;
Telo laesus, ense caesus, Sumerledus obiit...
Caput ducis infelicis Sumerledi clericus
Amputavit et donavit pontificis manibus.

("In the first onset the baneful duke fell; wounded by a javelin, slain with the sword, died Somerled. A cleric cut off the luckless leader's head and gave it into the bishop's hands"). In that sharp reversion to ancient head-hunting there is something befitting the end of one who had always been larger than life.

Some say King Malcolm sent the body to Iona, where many kings lie; but it was to the white sands of Saddell that his galley steered.

Among all the stones carved with ships and swords, mermaids and spearmen, none say *hic jacet Sumerledus rex insularum*. Those who knew needed no epitaphs; he will not be forgotten while MacDonalds and MacDougalls, MacRorys and MacAllisters, remember their roots.

The blows of fate have not flattened the grass. The sea-wind goes softly through branches where a blackbird sings; high above, a raven's croak rings like the clash of swords. It is a far cry to this green hollow from the Morvern cliffs, as far as from cave to crown.

10

The Mailed Fist

ALL SUMMER the cars rush north from Oban, making for Loch Awe or, by the cantilevered elbows of Connel Bridge, for the coast road to Ballachulish and the Great Glen. From either road a glance at the right moment may reveal one of the castles our visitors expect to see – Kilchurn crouching at Cruachan's feet, Stalker poised like a fairytale tower in the shallows west of the Strath of Appin. It is easy to miss an older castle within three miles of Oban; only when the trees are bare and the sun is low does a black cube rise like a clenched fist, beyond Dunbeg's white houses and the modern blockhouse of a Marine Research Station, on Dunstaffnage Bay.

If you thread your way through the village and past the laboratory, you will come to a carpark and a green lawn, and perched above it on a rock-boss a wall that grows so closely out of the boss that one can hardly tell where nature ends and skill began. It stands fast, secure against anything less than heavy artillery, to guard its bay where royal fleets have lain.

Offshore in the tiderace is a small island which looks as if it should be fortified (but apparently isn't) and just south of the castle is a ruined fort of unknown date, overlooking a chapel so elegant in its thirteenth-century detail as to proclaim itself a royal building. But first the castle, the mailed fist thrust sixty feet above the ground, commands all attention.

See how the living rock has been scarped below the foundations; look up to the white sandstone window-arches in the black walls, the gateway twenty feet up, with stone steps replacing the former timber stair and drawbridge, and ask yourself; is this some barbarian's attempt to ape his betters, a third-hand copy of ideas filtered from beyond the mountains, or is it the work of master masons under contract to a man who knew precisely what was the best of the time? Behind all strongholds, wherever they are, lies one of two basic ideas. Both go back to the earliest wandering men; a tree or a crag to climb, safe from wild beasts, or else a stockade – kraal of thorns, laager of wagons – to protect a band of travellers. Conquerors build sheer and small, like the prefabricated wooden towers the Normans ran up on earth-mounds in 1066; established groups need wider enclosures for families, stores and livestock. All strongpoints are altered through time, to take account of new methods of attack or defence, but behind each one stands the shadow of a man with his thumbs in his belt, saying to neighbours or followers, "We'll have to get organised before *they* appear," (whoever *they* may be), "and here's the place to fit the need."

Earlier 'experts' liked to think that advances in architecture, as in all else, spread very slowly into the wilds, that the simple Highlander was doomed to be behind the times, a prisoner of his mountains. But nobody is a prisoner with the sea at his door, no ship takes a century to voyage around Britain. Norsemen, accustomed to sailing from North Cape to Algiers, Vinland or Byzantium, pooled news and gossip at every anchorage; once they became integrated into the west-coast communities, local seamen could ship with them; from the days of Magnus Barefoot, and still more in Somerled's time, a powerful new magnet began pulling men south and eastward – the challenge of the Crusade.

The sheer size of the operations, the vast melting pot, the exchange of ideas within the crusading years, can slip out of mind as individual incidents take the spotlight. Every country of Christendom sent some troops for at least some campaigns, and stay-at-homes were kept aware of events through narratives of pilgrims or returned crusaders as well as by constant appeals for funds. Tales came back of eastern warfare, of mine and countermine, murderous heat and thirst, devilish secret weapons (something called 'Greek Fire' that burned faster the more you tried to douse it). In castle or hut the yarns were told: here we rode, hearing their drums all night, and here – this knife is our column – here, they broke through a pass above us, and messire Tancred bade sound the trumpets…

Anyone thinking of castle building from 1100 onwards would be foolish not to inquire into the latest defence works of Syria; certainly any attacker would know any new notions. In most countries a knight could not run up a stone tower without his overlord's consent, or he might find himself pulling it down again like any modern builder who forgets about planning permission; but on the western fringe of Scotland the King of Scots' writ hardly ran.

The quarrelsome Sons of Somerled tore his realm to shreds and set themselves grimly down to hold what they had and, on any opportunity, to filch more from an unwary kinsman. Here and there castles rose – Castle Sween, on the Knapdale shore, probably the first and perhaps built for Suibhne, one of the Úi Néill kin, rather than a Son. All up the coast castles began to sprout, to guard ships, stores and dependents. The oldest bear a marked family resemblance; maybe the masons travelled from one to the next. They all share ideas; a great courtyard to hold cattle and people, an upstairs door and a retractable ladder to admit late arriving crewmen with the pursuit at their heels.

Dunstaffnage had the high entrance but not the accessible courtyard (as it seems; we don't know how negotiable the former drawbridge may have been), but on the cliff above Oban Bay stands a sister castle to meet all needs. Dunollie is at least as old as Dunstaffnage, probably older. Its name crops up in chronicles of war between Dalriadic rivals or with the Picts. Tradition also links Dunstaffnage with those days, claiming that the Stone of Destiny rested there for a time; it was likely so to do, while the kingship swung between branches of the *rig-domna*. Dugald Somerledsson, establishing his base at Dunstaffnage, or Dunollie where his descendants live today, was proclaiming his descent from ancient kings.

Duncan his son sought Scottish help against his relatives and gave feudal homage to William the Lion in exchange for the title of *Dominus Ergadiae*, Lord of Argyll. Dugald himself had been to York with King William in 1175; perhaps the white sandstone arches of Dunstaffnage reflect a memory of York's city walls.

With his eastern flank secured and his island holding settling into a peace of sorts, Duncan could help the next king tighten his grip over the wilder west and even move so far with the times as to erect a Valliscaulian priory at Ardchattan. But if the isles were more peaceful, Scotland and Norway were on a collision course and the island kinglets had new anxieties to drive their castle works.

Alexander II had decided to exert his rights throughout his realm. In Norway Haakon IV came from nothing – illegitimate, posthumous, snatched from a choir-school in childhood by a jarl who meant to make him a puppet king. That jarl found to his cost that the boy was no puppet;

Haakon grew so strong that even republican Iceland and distant Greenland sought his help. No sooner was he master of Norway than he began looking to the lost western empire. An abortive expedition in 1229-30 only helped Alexander's plans, but when Duncan of Argyll died and his son Eòghann succeeded, Haakon was ready.

In summer 1248 Eòghann was summoned to Norway, with his cousin Dugald MacRuaraidh of the North Isles and their cousin King Harald of Man. All three were to receive their crowns from their overlord, and Harald was to marry one of Haakon's daughters (presumably Eòghann had been to the Scots court and obtained leave of absence from his mainland fief). Despite the ill omen of a disastrous palace fire, the wedding went smoothly and the happy couple set sail. Soon after came the news that they and all their people had been lost at sea.

When news of the wreck in Sumburgh Roost reached Haakon, he appointed Eòghann his viceroy for Man and the Isles, bidding him leave by the first ship of spring; Dugald MacRuaraidh remained in Norway and did not see his isles for fourteen years. Eòghann brought the news of King Harald's death to Man, saw Harald's brother enthroned, and prudently took the remaining Manx prince home with him to Argyll. So far, so good; but he can have had few illusions about the difficulties of keeping the peace until a Norwegian fleet could arrive.

Like any sensible thirteenth-century vassal he turned to his other overlord. He was straddling two worlds, on one side the virtually classless, independent-minded, islanders – on the other the stratified feudal state the Scots kings were trying to build. Feudal rules were clear; a vassal's loyalty was given in exchange for lands adequate to supply a specified tally of fighting men, for a set period (weeks rather than months). Conversely the overlord owed the vassal his backing. If Alexander would put garrisons into Eòghann's mainland castles, Eòghann's own men could be deployed to police the Isles.

But Alexander was angry, perhaps over Eòghann's acceptance of the viceroyalty without consultation, perhaps because he was already seeking a *casus belli*. Instead of support troops he set out himself, on a war cruise thinly disguised as a pilgrimage to Iona and a state visit to attend the installation of the new bishop of Argyll in Lismore; and he ordered Eòghann to surrender four castles beyond Scotland. (The only identifiable one is Cairnburgh Mór in the Treshnish Isles; Dùn Chonnaill in the Garvellachs is a distinct probability; Mingary or Duart or Aros are possibilities, as is the 'exceedingly strong tower' which Fordoun found in Tiree and which has now vanished).

Eòghann heard nothing of Norwegian reinforcements, but he did learn that the King of Man he enthroned in May had been assassinated in June. Only in early July did a boat escape with the news. The boy Magnus was now sole heir to Man, followed by Eòghann himself by descent from Somerled's Ragnhild. There was no knowing how close the Manx killers might be; Eòghann whisked the boy to safety in the Isle of Lewis.

When Alexander came sailing up the channel between green Kerrera and the red cliffs of Gallanach he found no humbly-waiting vassal. July can be sultry; the King was probably in full fig of chainmail and robes; we know also that he suffered from a severe allergy to fish (so much so that he had papal permission to keep Lent with cheese and vegetables instead). There are always troublemakers to stir a hot tempered man to wrath, and Alexander had his family's red hair. However it happened, the royal council did a bit of business, put off the Lismore visit, hung around discussing maybe seizing Eòghann's castles themselves.

By nightfall there was no such talk; the King was dead. There are two remarkable things about that death; firstly, in a time when every sudden death and most lingering ones were put down to witchcraft, poison or both, nobody dropped dark hints about the fifty-one-year-old King. Secondly, five days later they enthroned their next king at Scone.

Five days. Five days from Kerrera to Perthshire, summoning earls and barons and bishops, fetching the seven-year-old Prince Alexander from wherever he had been left with his mother, conveying the late King's body to his waiting tomb in Melrose – it throws light on the standard of communications in thirteenth-century Scotland.

So young a child had never before been enthroned, though unhappily there were to be others still younger in future. Factions and feuds wracked the country; Eòghann's troubles were swept aside and he struggled alone to keep the peace for two kings and bring a third to his throne. Fourteen years on, when he came back into the reckoning, he was still serving two masters.

Alexander III pursued his father's plan to buy the Isles from Haakon, a sensible proposal which offended the old man immensely. He reacted by building a war fleet and in 1263 brought it slowly through the Isles, anchoring in Oban Bay, sweeping on past Islay and Gigha, round Kintyre and into the Clyde, summoning liegemen and taking tribute of food and stores. Eòghann went back and forth between Haakon and Alexander, vainly trying to patch up a settlement. Despite his efforts, ships and army confronted each other on the Clyde near Largs, where the Michaelmas storms did more than the Scots could to rout the invaders.

By the end of Alexander's reign, a time later Scots wistfully called 'the time of peace', Norway had ceded him all the Western Isles and Man had submitted to him also. For a brief moment it looked as if the two realms would unite under his grandchild Margaret, Princess of Norway, Queen of Scots, already proposed as bride for Edward I's infant son. But that was not to be; the last moments of the Time of Peace came with the Maid of Norway's death, and darkness fell upon Scotland.

Dusk might have drawn down sooner if one man had not kept the west. The castles of the island coasts, and black Dunstaffnage, the keystone of that arch, are fit monuments to Eòghann of Argyll, man of two worlds.

11

Midwinter

WHEN THE soldiers had gone she went out to the peatstack. Gilbert's flail was thudding again in the barn, venting his helpless anger. A few dry snowflakes brushed her cheek; the ice at the ford crackled under the hooves of the sergeant's pony; the outermost peats were frozen together. The short January day was drawing to frost as the sun dipped into rosy mists beyond Islay, but there were streaks of bare grass on the braes and tomorrow, maybe, the iron cold would ease.

Her eyes followed the search party – one riding, four trudging with hoods pulled close and spears gripped under cloaks. The Black Man wi them for the mess they'd left! But for all their wrastling they had missed the flat stone in the back wall of the byre…maybe they'd come by chance after all. Well, she'd need to put the house to rights.

That was when she saw the other man.

Her heart jolted. Mary Mother, a stranger in the glen, in this weather? He'd walk slap into the soldiers at the bend of the brae, and she with no way to warn him! Her arms full of peats, she stood and shook with more than cold.

He padded steadily onward. He did not care to be so nakedly obvious, for he had learned long ago than a man alone is more noteworthy than a few lads together. He'd had friends, old or new, beside him all winter in the caves or the boats. Coming from the shore today he'd taken one end of a pole loaded with fish, and when the patrol overtook them Dugald had given them the universal nod and "Aye-aye, cauld day!", but there was no possible reason to bring Dugald on past his cousin's house, and so he was here on his own. It would be equally fatal to hurry or to skulk; he must be just a surly fellow going home if he met that patrol returning. He did not like to think where they might have been – but at least there was no thatch-smoke coiling up into the quiet dusk.

He didn't feel surly. He felt alive and alert as he had not been all winter. It was like the first time his grandfather had put him up on the old bay charger; "Up with you – brat, and let's see what you've learnt." Aye, up with us, and we'll show them; what's the use of worrying? They know what's to do, my job is to be there at the right time.

But still he was uneasy. He misliked this business of marching up to a strange house and asking to be piloted through the hills. It wasn't as if they had been able to forewarn the man. From the look of this country he could have found his own way, and maybe he'd best do just that after all.

A hoof clinked on ice, and he stepped off the path as the patrol rounded the rocks. He grunted "Cauld nicht!" with his chin in his plaid and stood glum and blank-eyed in the heather.

As soon as the woman saw him come round the corner she ran into the barn.

"Gilbert – here a man coming – they let him by – come till you see if you know him!"

"Ach, be easy, it'll be some travelling body. Put you the broth to heat while I go down and meet him."

"*A'Dhia*, hadn't we our troubles today already? It's a wonder they left us the broth itself!"

She went back to tackle her wrecked kitchen. They had rummaged through all her store-kists, thrust their spears into woolbags, tossed blankets on the earth floor, made a right *bourach* of every place...and for what? It had been no ordinary arms-search, they'd been after something big, as big as a man maybe; but nobody had slept in the wall hole this side of Michaelmas. She muttered angrily as she worked, all the words she had bitten back for fear they'd throw the hearthfire into the thatch for sheer spite.

She wiped her face with her apron when she heard the two men at the door. The stranger came in first.

"God save all here!"

"God save you kindly, come away in, it's a snell day to be walking. You'll take a drop of broth?"

"My word, a fire's a grand sight. And you had the soldiers, Mem? You would think they could find an easier job in this weather. I was telling Himself here, they call me Raibeart and I've to go a message to Arran."

She relaxed a little, not entirely. No great danger in a man going eastward, but his wariness drew answering caution from her. Still, the duties of hospitality were clear.

"Not past this door tonight! Gilbert will put you on the road in the morning if the snow holds off. Will it be Saddell he wants, Gilbert?"

"I was thinking maybe Duncan in Ugadale might have the curach out, seeing it's quiet weather."

Not Saddell; so Gilbert knew this was another of the secret men; there were overmany watchful eyes about Saddell Abbey.

"Aye, quiet weather; coming from Cara the day we'd a few flurries of snow, just. Mind you, when we crossed from Jura it was wild altogether."

Now he was telling them too much and they all knew it. She would never question a guest, and he ought not to burden her with any knowledge. She watched him as he sat by the hearth; he'd an odd lilt to his Gaelic, and yon rough cloak was some Islay woman's weaving. A prickle of apprehension still troubled her; could he be a spy, this upstanding man with the laugh in the brown eyes of him? Some woman would be blithe to see him home.

He was asking Gilbert the news of the countryside when her Gift fell suddenly upon her. The peat smoke seemed to part and show her a row of bars, and behind them a girl child crouched on flagstones and holding a cloak about her with frozen little hands. *Mary pity the wean, and she a king's daughter!* The smoke thickened; with anger shaking her she glanced quickly at the men, but they hadn't noticed. She'd maybe tell Gilbert later, once he was safely home again, but now was no time to stir grief and anger.

"I'll just take these blankets straight through to the other place," she said, gathering an armful from the corner. Gilbert quirked an eyebrow and nodded. She went away raging inwardly; what manner of devil put a wee lass in a cage like yon? Someone had said the Lady o'Buchan was penned up like a caged songbird on a wall, just for setting a crown on the rightful king's head; aye, but some day – some day...

She was cooler when she returned, and just as well too, for they had worked round to things that never came out except when doors were safely steeked.

"So, what word of him they used to call Earl of Carrick?"

"No word this long time," said Gilbert. "I was hearing he was in Ireland a while ago. There's some folk give him another name, friend."

"Aye, likely; he's had a few names, yon one. Is it good or bad, the name he gets in Kintyre?"

"It'll depend who's speaking," said Gilbert, grinning.

"I warrant you, and who's listening! Has anyone a kind word for him?"

"Just this, that he came out of England saying he *maun be wi' his ain folk*. That's the talk for the likes of me."

Gilbert my brave fool, haven't enough folk heard you yet? Isn't that what brought the soldiers here? But the stranger was on his feet.

"My hand in yours, friend, and here's to Scotland yet!"

When they had him snugly bedded in the nest of hay and blankets, in the hole dug into the slope, and had eased the stone into place and brought the cow, grumbling, back to her stall, Gilbert went out to the door. There was a blaze of stars, but at the glen-head they were dimmed by the leap and flicker of the Northern Lights.

"The Clever Men are dancing, wife; we'll see blood on the stones by morning!"

He meant the lichen that flames red after frost, *fuil na sluaigh*, the blood of the army in the sky; but Annag shivered:

"My sorrow on the wars!"

She woke suddenly, feeling him slide out of bed.

"Is it that time? Open the fire till I heat something for you. Promise me you'll take care? You don't know who goes with you."

"Never fear, lass. If you're asked, I'm away to the hill for a barren hind and I'll not be back till I get one. Put us up a bannock or two, there's a long road ahead of him. I'll away and waken him."

The stranger roused instantly at the first sound in the byre, and slid out on his feet, bright-eyed. The kitchen glowed with firelight, the porridge glucking and Annag knotting oatcakes and cheese into a cloth.

The men went uphill on crisped grass under enormous stars. Once a grouse whirred off downwind, once they heard afar a vixen's eerie scream. They climbed the long slopes southerly, skirting drifts. The stranger crouched suddenly, gripping Gilbert's arm, on the glimpse of a tall shape like a listening sentry. Gilbert chuckled:

"I should have minded to warn you – it's just an old Giant's Stone. The way's mostly downhill from this; the first two waters run to Saddell Glen but the third brings us right to Ugadale."

As they went forward the vast bulk of Arran began to take shape in the east. The sky was bleaching, a faint flush spread and against it that well remembered ridge stood crisp and dark. Far below them the sea glinted. It was full morning before they reached a wind-bent thicket above the shore.

"We'll take a bite here before I go down and speak to Duncan. Let you bide till I come for you. Yon's Machrie Bay over the water, and that's where he'll land you. It's nigh ten miles from there to Brodick, but he'll tell you how to find a man that'll see you right."

Gilbert slipped away and presently emerged striding across fields towards a house under the hill. The man called Raibeart settled himself to wait. He ran his eye over the coast below, studying the cover (or lack of it), seeking likely corners for a lurking watcher. Presently he made out a dark something a bit to southward; now, he thought, if I were set to guard this shore, that's where I'd be; it's some old stronghold, and they have ever a good outlook.

A wisp of smoke was rising behind its wall; someone was making breakfast. A cold wind blew from Carrick, and whoever was posted in the fort had no mind to face it – though he might be looking downwind instead. I'd have had a man on the wall, or stood there myself, wind or no wind, unless – nasty thought – there were hidden loopholes in the wall. Ah well, Gilbert must know the risks.

And over there, in the eye of the wind, lay home. He must be looking right at Turnberry, now in enemy hands, with all its memories of his forceful mother and his pliant father and the old grandfather – old hero, old Crusader, old tyrant – God, how he had loved that man! But here came Gilbert MacKay again.

They kept well clear of the fort, making for the north side of the point and halting among scrub oaks just above the last steep pitch, beside a big flat rock in a clearing.

"Well, here's me away back now. Just you go on down through those hazels and you'll find Duncan with the boat ready. Fare ye well, and here's to good times coming."

"Bide one moment – put this in your pouch. Go on, man, would I insult you with money? It's just a bit brooch – bring it to me when the good times come and I'll maybe find a way to thank you."

"I'd liefer have a kiss of my king's hand," said Gilbert, and knelt.

"Blessed saints, how came I to put you in such jeopardy! How did you know me?"

"Ach, never heed; I've been at Carrick Fair in my time. Away you go now, Duncan's waiting. It's no' a bad day at all."

He turned quickly uphill, and the man Raibeart, in other times and places sometimes called *messire Robert de Brus, Comte de Carric*, and elsewhere *Rex Scottorum*, slithered downhill to the coracle.

12

Roebuck and Comet

THERE ARE people whose life can be summed up in one act of courage or faith or fear, and others who cram so much into one lifespan as to leave common mortals aghast. So too there are places distinguished by one building, one hill, one tree against the sunset – and others that have beauty, history, flowers, birdsong, and people to enjoy them.

Where the sea cuts deep into the land it is all the better for some islands; a wide valley is enhanced by a few fine trees; nobody knew better than an eighteenth-century architect where to place a stately house. A narrowing gorge into trackless country is ready primed with mystery, and it would be a pity if no magic lay in its custody.

The seaward end of Loch Craignish opens upon the *Dorus Mór*, the Big Door whose tiderips can bolt and bar it against all comers. The islands stand aside to leave clear passage to the loch's head where Barbreck House stands serene with Highland cattle at rest under the park trees, conveying the impression of a well-composed landscape sharpened by a Prospect of Horrid Mountains, the steep valley flanks as artificial as a Grotto or a Gothick Ruin.

Behind the house the strath begins to shrink until a line of crags juts into the path of the river, closing off the green fields and hiding the upper glen behind a brown shoulder. Here begins Glen Domhain, the deep one; here the grey wagtails flitter and the buzzards plane and mew, and on the stillest day there is always the faint sound of rock screes moving. The path up the waterside is almost invisible when you are on it, though the eye picks out its twisting thread through rocks upstream.

It is not a long glen, under three miles from the road-end at Turnalt to the Dalavich road near ruined Lagalochan, but I know no other that carries one so far from the present. Near its head, hard to spot on a low heathery mound, lies a small flat stone carved with the outline of a deer.

It's difficult to explain exactly how to find it; now that some bright modern Ostrogoth (may its transistor blow up in its ear) has left its initials on the stone, I am disinclined to try. It used to be marked by a sherd of drainpipe, and only the shepherds saw it and pondered. It's called a 'roebuck' but the antlers are not quite right; one romantic reporter claimed it was a 'reindeer' and marked 'where the last of the breed was killed'. Since this event may well have occurred before even hunting man trod these braes, and since the carving has been engraved with a sharp metal tool, that theory must seem improbable; in any case the horns and the head carriage are both wrong. Nobody has dated it for certain, nobody really knows why it is there; long may it guard its lonely pass.

To return down the glen is to move through time. There are cairns and cist-graves below Turnalt, the remains of one stone circle and the site of another close to Barbreck itself. A mausoleum of dead admirals and generals stands ruinous on a mound called *Dùnan Aula* (or *Amlaibh*; Olaf's Hillock), where local tradition says the natives routed 'Danish' invaders. The masons who built the mausoleum uncovered a Bronze Age grave and smashed its 'pot of gold' to find 'only the dust of Olaf' (and serve them right).

The odd thing is that the Saga of Olaf Tryggvesson records that, in the 980s before he ruled Norway, King Olaf raided west-over-sea; and Irish annals say many of his men were cut off in Dalriada, killed or sold into slavery. 'Danes' is the nineteenth-century word for *Lochlannaich*, the Gaelic term for any Viking raiders; those who wrote local histories such as entries for the two *Statistical Accounts* anxiously coloured them to polite English usage, avoiding barbarous Scotticisms. Thus the parish minister who tells of Olaf goes on to speculate about an Anglo-Saxon meaning ('slaughter') for nearby Sluggan; a straightforward Gaelic 'hollow' would have been less acceptable. (Just why the site of a Danish defeat should be marked by a Saxon placename is something only the reverend gentleman could have explained).

There is also a 'Danish King's Grave' high on the flank of the hill down which the road from Lochgilphead plunges to the valley floor. This, too, is a prehistoric site, at least two cairns and a great standing stone. The fertile strath has drawn many raiders, and many are the small forts tucked into the hills or poised above landing places. There are old church sites too, Kilbride of Turnalt hidden from the sea, Kilmory (or possibly Kilmoire, 'Mary's Church' which some people call Kilvaree – though when Kil-names were formed, they usually referred to some missionary founder), still the Kirkton, its walls guarding a rich hoard of carved gravestones; near Aird Farm, a tiny grassgrown *cille* so old that its dedication is lost. In a low gravelbank near the Kirkton a whole Bronze Age cemetery was uncovered by roadmakers; in one cist there was neither spear nor axehead but a pot crammed with reddish hair. It was once thought to be human, the grave gift of some mourning woman; now it is reported to be cow's hair, whatever that tells us about burial practices – and perhaps early specimens of Highland cattle.

Craignish is full of signals from the past, cupmarked rocks and one stone with a strange symbol to which small crosses have been added, presumably to cancel a pagan intention. When a bold farmer took that slab for a door lintel, a voice came nightly to ask for its return – not threatening, just softly begging to have its own again. It was duly returned to its mound and the voice was stilled.

Another voice used to be heard; between the main road and the burn on the western edge of the Big House grounds, a little upright stone stands by a well. It looks like any eighteenth-century gravestone, a small bewigged head at the top, and front, back and edges covered with an inscription. The lettering, decent mason's capitals with an N or two reversed, is hard to decipher but luckily it was copied while it was more legible:

my.name.is.watchman.heir.am.I.still.
watching.day.andnight.welcoming.al.
persons.that.comes.heir.to.drink.

and so on, ending with:'iiird March 1734.this.al.by.Barbreck.'

Watchman – who must surely have lived in the well before his stone was carved – used to converse with his callers, until the Campbells left Barbreck and took him with them; again, his voice troubled them until they returned his stone, but he has never spoken since.

A gentle place, then? A place of friendly voices and old magic? Well, yes – and no. Beyond Kirkton the square bulk of Craignish Castle stares seaward, still inhabited but so old that it needed repairs in 1414, when one Ranald Campbell held it for the service of a sea-going galley. The clifftop fort that frowns towards the Kirkton gravelpit was manned by militiamen in 1746, and in the years between those dates there had been some wild doings.

We owe our knowledge of them to a douce Scots lawyer, Alexander Campbell of the Craignish line, who sat down early in the eighteenth century to collect all he knew of his ancestors. Beginning with Paul of the Sporran, purse-bearer to Duncan I (whom MacBeth slew), and bypassing a sprig of the family tree transplanted to Breadalbane –"a black and bloody headstrong race they were, I have seen some of them" – he gossips of murder, raid and rapine as if to prove the antiquity of his descent by the volume of blood spilt. He revels in a row over a dowry, which led to unarmed men being hunted home from Kilneuair Church on Loch Awe until they turned on their pursuers with alder clubs at a ford; he gives gory details of the slaying of a six-year-old boy by his foster father (the most sacred relationship in Gaeldom) because the child talked of revenging his own father, killed by the fosterer's foster brother; and he trims his quill and rubs his hands when he comes to Ranald's Aunt Christian, the White Lady of Craignish.

How sweet she sounds, a dear little old lavender-scented soul, no doubt. You wait. She flourished in the mid-fourteenth century. As her father's heiress, her marriage was of course arranged; the chosen bridegroom was a MacDougall of Lorn, proof enough that her family paid little regard to their own chiefs – the Loch Awe Campbells had been at feud with the Dunollie MacDougalls since the wars of Robert Bruce, a generation earlier. A MacDougall wife for twenty years, mother of a MacDougall son, the White Lady was no sooner widowed than she wed to please herself.

Her choice fell on a cousin on the mother's side, a MacNaughton from Loch Aweside. Her Campbell uncle thought the match unworthy of her. A year later the bridegroom died (the uncle's connection is not explicit) and Christian, riding down Glen Domhain in her widow's weeds, encountered a young McIver from Arduaine. In that glen, now all desolate and treeless, there was then a small wood, later to be called the Lady's – *Coille na Bhain-tighearna*; that was where the white widow seduced her mate.

All the kinsmen were furious, even to the point of seeking the help of their much neglected overlord. Campbell of Loch Awe did indeed compel her to buy her right of re-marriage, but she merrily gave him the whole strath of Barbreck and a slice of MacNaughton land forbye, so that all the protesters obtained was the loss of large chunks of territory.

At last she died; but one could hardly hope that was the end of trouble. Four principal families attended the funeral – Campbells, MacDougalls, MacNaughtons and MacIvers. Alexander the lawyer assumed they came to hear the will read, but there were few testaments and fewer family lawyers in Christian's day. The Campbells and MacIvers set off with the coffin for Kilmory; the MacDougalls protested that her place was in their church of Kilbride at Lerags. The MacNaughtons hung back discreetly (in all this there is the hint of a novel kind of *habeas corpus*, as if those who interred the body could somehow claim the possessions).

They halted for refreshments at a convenient barn. By sheer mishap, (of course), the barn door jammed with the MacDougalls on the inside, and before they could break through the wall the other mourners had vanished. The coffin was still quite near, had they known where to look; it had been tucked under the capstone of a cist that still stands on Soroba Farm. The MacDougalls wasted no time playing find-the-lady, but whipped up as many Craignish cattle as a rapid sweep revealed, and drove them up the Bealach Mór. (This was the long way home, but avoided MacIver land.)

The rest of the funeral party pursued them hotfoot, except for the patient MacNaughtons who emerged from cover and bore the coffin away up Glen Domhain.

There was lots more lovely mayhem to be told, and none of it worried the respectable old gentleman in his wing chair. Should he record the recent splendid row about a site for the new manse and glebe? Possibly not; there might be further litigation; but he could safely enlarge on the troubles of his distant cousin the Baron of Barrichbeyan, a small laird who had tried to compel his tenants to reap his crop before their own. He was strong, and they were but poor helpless folk; it was not for them to thwart the laird – but a right shame it was, such a grand drying wind ablowing and the oats standing white for the sickle... But wait you now, man; reap, Himself said; did you hear him say bind and stook too?

No, they agreed warily; Barrichbeyan was not saying we behoved to bind the sheaves. So they whetted their sickles, and they reaped. The fine wind blew day and night, and at the next dawning wasn't it the terrible pity that all yon grand corn was over the dyke into their own fields beyond?

What could they do but glean it all together, for how would anyone know which ear was his and which was ours? To the old byeword *Tenantry is stronger than landlord* was added a new one; "the reaping of the Baron of Barrichbeyan – shear today and sheaf tomorrow". The White Lady would have whooped – provided it was not her crop.

Old Alexander strayed happily among his bygone cattle thieves, his ancestors once the *Cheif Gaurdians of the Western Coast against Incursions of the Ilanders*; what would he have said if he had lived a few years longer, to see a vessel from beyond the wide Atlantic beating through the Dorus Mór? Would he have credited that a Scots-born seaman, named John Paul Jones, would dare bring his *Ranger* to prey on coastal shipping? Smuggling was something every gentleman approved – the notion of laying a duty upon snuff and claret must be repugnant to any man of feeling; but colonials turning privateer – whatever next?

What came next would really have dumbfounded him. Into the waters once patrolled by Ranald's galley came a new sound and sight, throbbing and thumping and belching of smoke. Out of Crinan crept Bell's little *Comet*, outclassed on the Clyde by her successors and bravely tackling seas too fierce for her. Lengthened to carry more cargo, all through 1820 she trudged valiantly between Fort William and Glasgow by way of the Crinan Canal. Even the music of her piper, one Donald MacDougall (engaged at six shillings a week and his food) could not entice enough passengers to pay her way. At last she struggled out of Oban in a December snowstorm, her pumps fighting a leak, and met her fate in the Dorus Mór.

The wreck of the world's first sea going steamship lay on the tip end of Craignish, the hull broken at the point of lengthening and the engines jammed among the rocks. Salvage proved impossible, even after the expenditure of £5.18.6d on whisky for the rescuers. Just across the bay lay Crinan, with safety in its sea lock. From the Roebuck of Glen Domhain to Henry Bell's *Comet* is a long step. Today, if the Barrichbeyan fields are cropped at all they are reaped by combine and the only White Ladies are Whooper swans moving slowly through the Barfad shallows and talking softly of northern seas. Still the keep of Craignish stands foursquare and standing stones point towards the stars. Below the castle a grove of alien tree-ferns rustles, whispering of distant places and days long gone by.

13

Islay of the Kings

FROM THE mainland it glows with an inner light, like a piece of uncut amethyst laid on the sea, now forming one long serrated jewel with its neighbour Jura, or again set, by a trick of the light, behind Brosedale and a silver thread of inlay marking the Sound of Islay. The three cones of the Paps of Jura are more readily recognised – from the Irish cliffs, even on a rare day from the tower of Glasgow University – but Islay has its own distinctive outline:

See afar yon hill Ardmore

on an air to catch the heart, at a city ceilidh or from a man working at his nets.

Every isle – almost every headland and township in the isles – has its praise song, too often its song of parting, but *In Praise of Islay* rallies exiles worldwide. Yet, as the ship draws nearer, the island turns a bleak shoulder. Northward lies the greenest corner of Jura, guarded by the island castle of Fraoch Eilean and backed by the soaring Paps; southward the voyager confronts dark cliffs with a lighthouse clinging perilously, scree streaked hills scored by barren valleys. The ferry bustles through the tide-race towards a cleft where white houses flatten themselves against the rocks; as she swings for the pier there is a glimpse of Colonsay, low and blue to the west beyond Rudh'a'Mhail.

There are woods at Port Askaig, full of birdsong and bright with young leaves, through which the road climbs in bold corkscrews – a fitting introduction to the home of the Islay Malts – to reach broad grasslands. The farther you go, the richer the farms, down to Bridgend and the sweep of Loch Indaal. Here is the hidden heart of the rich island, wide silvery waters where the wild duck rest and myriads of waders lift and pipe, a hidden world, an isle apart.

It has been a land of promise from the earliest times; today it is among the richest corners of Britain and yields thousands of pounds for every man, woman and babe-in-arms to the London Treasury, so that Lagavullin and Caol-Ila, Laphroaig and Bruichladdich, are music in southern ears (or would be, if they could pronounce them). An odd local preference for large dark buildings topped by something like pagoda towers will gradually explain itself, after a few conducted tours of such magical palaces.

The island has also been a thorn in the side of kings, a centre of resistance, holding its own parliament in medieval times and again as lately as last century, but today it is chiefly famed for its whiskies and its armies of birds.

Here the wild geese drop from sunset skies in long singing skeins, with a clamour of wings like the roar of battle. Here choughs soar above the cliffs, godwits and sanderlings flit along the sands, woodcock croak at dusk, every bush has its small songster. Birdwatchers creep among the dunes, and so do the archaeologists, for the dunes are restless and lay bare old bones and long-hidden swords. Up in the hills, a peatslip reveals miniscule slivers of white flint, chipped eight thousand years ago to arm a hunter's spear.

It is an enchanted island and casts a swift spell. Here the Norsemen settled more densely than in any other of the Sudreys. The island geography echoes in miniature the components of the old lost Kingdom of the Isles. Its northern and eastern sides are as bleak as the Rough Bounds beyond Ardnamurchan; the north-west recalls the scalped peat wastes of the Outer Isles; the Rhinns look to Ireland. The Mull of Oa, the southern headland where choughs cry, is like the Isle of Man with its small square fields and its farmsteads snugly tucked into hill folds.

At the north edge of the Oa a massive stone marks the death spot of Godred of the White Hand, Gorry Crovan, King Orry of Man. It overlooks the length of Laggan Bay, past the airfield and the golf course to the peat cuttings that feed the distilleries and the mighty golden dunes where dead Vikings sleep.

Before the Norsemen came the Irish preachers, marking their steps with crosses from Kildalton the magnificent to little Kilnave, so slender that its arms seem to quiver in the winds of ocean. The first tiny churches fell prey to the Norse, but later generations rebuilt them and lie within their ruins, under stones carved with ships and swords and armoured knights. In a green cup of the hills lies a silver lake set with islets, where stood the castle that ruled all the Isles, a chapel where kings and queens worshipped, an island where Councils met, and a stone on which each new Lord of the Isles set his foot. Here, to Finlaggan, fate brought in the year 1400 as strange an exile as Islay ever welcomed.

The Lord of the Isles in that day was Donald, nephew of the King of Scots, far stronger in his own realm than his enfeebled uncle. He could afford to go his own way, ignoring King Robert III, travelling abroad (he was a graduate of Oxford), making his own treaties with Richard II of England (Table 4, p.215 may be useful here).

He often looked in at Richard's court, and when Henry IV seized power Donald was among the first to visit him. He may even have watched the ex-king's funeral procession move up Cheapside to St Paul's, though neither Donald nor any other great man chose to follow the coffin to its obscure grave in the Dominican Priory of Langley. Donald was busy instead negotiating a new treaty with the usurper. He got home to find Finlaggan buzzing with strange speculations.

Like any other medieval potentate, the Lord of the Isles was a magnet for unfortunates; it was part of his glory to feed the hungry and befriend the friendless. Any poor crazed creature landing from a Welsh ship would be led to Finlaggan as a matter of course.

In Finlaggan, while Donald went overseas, there remained his wife, his brother John the Tanist (the chosen vice-chief under Gaelic law), and John's wife, an Irish lady who had met King Richard in Ireland during his last disastrous campaign. She and John had seen Richard as the end approached, half-distraught and heading for the breakdown that helped Henry to the throne; they had known him, too, in happier times, elegant and fantastical, with the slender hands and the delicate face below the red-gold hair, familiar even now from portraits – a face one does not readily forget. It was the Lady Marjory who first voiced an extraordinary suspicion.

The more she looked at the newly arrived scarecrow, the surer she became. It was no good trying to laugh her out of the conviction that here stood King Richard, out of his right mind maybe, and no wonder if all one heard was true, but alive. Nor was she the only one to entertain such notions; Donald's court jester sat sulking, half jealous of a rival, half awed by fate's trickery.

Meanwhile the man from the ship lay by the hearth, picking at his new cloak, spreading his long fingers to the warmth – and wept. He had no name for himself, or would not tell it. The watchers sometimes heard him plead with invisible companions; sometimes when the harps were struck he rose with a strange dignity and moved to table first of all the paupers.

They tried all the tricks – sudden questions, courteous enquiries – in vain. As the chronicler Wyntoun later wrote:

> Quether he had bene King or nane
> Thare was but few that wist certane.
> Of devotion nane he was,
> And seldom will had to hear Mass;
> As he bare him, like was he
> Often half wodd or wild to be...

But nobody could fail to see in him Plantagenet. It was common knowledge that the Black Prince had left more sons than one, and that Richard had used stand-ins through boring ceremonies; King Henry was steadily accounting for them as for anyone who mentioned usurpers or sighed for past times. Donald knew all that, but through time and against his better judgment he became convinced that he was housing neither a stand-in nor a bastard brother of the deposed King of England. He wrote to his uncle to announce that Islay held a very strange guest.

He took care not to assert positively that Richard had escaped from Pomfret and its murder squad; the ink was barely dry on his new treaty with Henry IV. He merely stated the bare truth – he had a madman who looked more like the ex-king than was reasonable, and he was sending the creature to Ayrshire, *en route* for Stirling and King Robert's advisers. He would travel as the 'Mammet of Islay' – Islay's doll or simulacrum or puppet; and a puppet he would remain for twenty years.

Robert III was old; long before his accession he had been crippled by a horse's kick, and had now virtually abandoned the conduct of affairs to his brother the Duke of Albany. It was Albany who dealt with the Mammet, housing him honourably in Stirling Castle, assembling a pitiful gathering of Richard's ex-followers who had taken refuge in France, even discovering a personal seal which shortly appeared on letters sent into England. Albany was the ablest politician of his day, and knew an asset when he saw one. Curious things had a way of happening around him, such as the death of Robert's eldest son the Duke of Rothesay, and the capture at sea of the second prince, James, on his way to France in time of truce, by chance encounter with an English ship. The shock of James's capture was too much for his old father; Albany was soon sole Regent for a child king imprisoned at Windsor.

If only Shakespeare had stumbled upon this tale; if only, between *King Lear* and *MacBeth*, he had given us a *Richard II, Part 2*, with a king whose divinity shone through madness, the ruler of an enchanted isle to befriend him, a Fool for philosophical whimsy, a usurping Regent with a restless conscience...

James VI and I would not relish too favourable a portrait of Donald, whose heirs were out of royal favour, but the main theme must have pleased him. In his view monarchs were unalterably divine; and a Stewart was to rescue the sufferer.

There could be links with earlier works. Harry Hotspur, arguably the dramatist's favourite, had died in a rebellion caused by Henry IV's refusal to let him claim ransom for Albany's son Murdoch, but Hotspur's old father and young son found refuge in Scotland (*Act III, Scene 1; a room in Stirling Castle; enter Northumberland and Henry Percy*, with a suitable selection of Scottish lords).

Wales was aflame under Hotspur's old sparring partner Owen Glendower (*"I can call spirits from the vasty deep..."*) and afire with rumours that King Richard lived. Such stories follow many great men's fall; one need look no farther than the Berlin Bunker. Established rulers laugh at such tales, but Henry could not afford the luxury of mercy. Among his victims were eight Franciscan friars who had hinted that they knew how Richard escaped (his red-gold head muffled in a grey hood? No record was kept of the friars' lies). Anyone caught repeating the story was doomed; even the Archbishop of Canterbury was soundly snubbed for suggesting one might at least send someone to inspect the Mammet before issuing official denials.

Albany could have bought his own son's freedom, and King James's, for the price of surrendering the Mammet or even of sending sure news of his death. He preferred to let Murdoch wait a little, and to keep his nephew off the throne by threats to confirm his pensioner's identity.

At last Henry V succeeded his father, and at once released young Murdoch. A further proposal to free King James was swiftly checked by hints of "bringing in the Mammet of Scotland to stir what he may". James must wait until Albany died, and by then the Regent's prisoner was also dead. They laid the Mammet to rest in the Blackfriars' Church, in the shadow of Stirling Rock, under a portrait and a long rhyming epitaph proclaiming him rightful King of England; when James's revenge fell on Murdoch, he and his sons lay on the other side of the same high altar. Altar and epitaph and church all vanished in the flames of the Reformation, so that we cannot know if the portrait showed an oval face and unforgettable hands; and it might be misleading to consider the choice of a Dominican church anything more than a coincidence with that shabby affair at Langley.

Yet suppose, for a moment, that the story had a kernel of truth; suppose the Mammet was Richard indeed. Did he struggle in the spider's web of Scottish politics, or rest content in the high Stirling chambers with the alien hills of the Highland Line standing sentinel to the North? Did the clouded mind ever clear, and did he remember the green island of his first refuge, where the surf thunders and the birds wheel and cry? *The setting sun and music at the close...the king shall be contented*.

Something like that might have made the curtain speech for Act V of *Richard II, the Second Part*; the rest is silence, and the sigh of an ebbing wave.

14

The Ships of Scotland

IN A MORE perfect world every local-government official, every Departmental Adviser or lifestyle-enhancer, would approach Argyll from the right end; at last a use for Clyde-based submarines suggests itself. All such well-intentioned persons would be conveyed underwater to Tiree and landed to begin their education.

They would learn that tide and weather are stronger than timetables; that map-distances are not the same as misty coasts half-seen; that while one can live without a daily paper, a fortnight's lack of meat and stock feed is less tolerable. At Gott Bay they could hear of the Boats of Scarinish.

A couple of centuries ago, as the women stood wringing their skirts dry after helping launch the fishing-boats, a white squall blanched the sea; when it cleared, there were no boats. Not a rope or an oar came ashore; they were widowed in one gust of wind. Months passed without means of sending word to Mull. At last some crews returned from Jura; a year later others arrived, having visited America aboard a clipper that had heard their hails. Of the rest, never a word.

Tiree is *Tìr fò Thuinn*, Land-Under-Wave, and lives by the sea's permission. Great tides have met across its waist, its tallest tree is a currant bush, at every gable a water-butt catches the precious rain under a sifting of sand. Terns nest on its airfield runways and from either side great lighthouse-beams sweep its skies.

Every second night the island passes the dark hours in ceilidh, ready to be down the pier at the back of five. The steamer thumps into the bay under a pearly sky, like a busy housewife drawing curtains. Cars bucket down the road, dogs bark, a rattle of Gaelic from the bridge is answered with mirth. Amid such untimely cheer the outsider stumbles up the gangway longing for a dark corner; he will do better to swallow his yawns, find the lee of a deckhouse, and watch the morning strengthen.

An expanse of grey silk ripples towards Mull. Iona is a smudge, Staffa a dark hump. As the ship turns north towards Coll, the pinky blockhouse of Breachacha Castle is watching.

Onwards from Arinagour she threads her course through a maze of headlands unfolding under the ribbed and milky cloudbanks. This is the way to make sense of Argyll's past; the sea is our highway, its surface broken by the sleek heads of seals and the fountain of a gannet's plunge or glinting with the black-white-black flash of a line of speeding shearwaters. Ahead looms the outermost western tip of Britain, the cliff of Ardnamurchan whose great torch blinks all night answering Skerryvore. Now the ship swings above a vast drowned crater, between Mull's basalt and Ardnamurchan's gabbro. The crest of Ben Hiant turns to gold, white houses stand toe-to-toe with their reflections, the grim grey bulk of Mingary Castle frowns.

The water moves as gently as a sleeper's breathing, not a ripple to recall storms or keels long-beached. Here came Iona brethren towing timber from Morvern, here swept dragon-prows, and a lost Armada galleon blundering in the toils of the Mull witches. Here too came those assiduous tourists Dr Samuel Johnson and Mr Boswell, inward-bound from Coll, Iona still to be worked into their schedule. Tobermory was a relief to Boswell:

> There are sometimes sixty or seventy sail here… To
> see such a fleet was the next best thing to seeing a town…
> After having been shut up so long in Col, the sight of such
> an assemblage of moving habitations, containing such a
> variety of people, engaged in different pursuits, gave me
> much gaiety of spirit.

Our newly liberated trainees might share his sentiments, moving through the Sound of Mull in a dance of kittiwakes with the water turning to sapphire as the mists smoke out of high glens. All the way we are overlooked, Breachacha handing us on to Mingary, Mingary to Dunara, Caisteal nan Con, then Ardtornish, then Duart. Allied or bristling with mutual jealousy, the castles have watched centuries pass.

For two hundred years after Haakon of Norway, no rival king challenged the Lords of the Isles. Their mighty Ardtornish is rubble now, but beyond Craignure a dark tower still wears its blazoned banner; MacLean is in Duart, overlooking the waters his clan galleys patrolled.

We cross the Firth of Lorne in a morning as blue as the saltire at our bows. To southward lie the Garvellachs like a squadron of warships; behind Oban, Cruachan lifts her lovely head; far up the Firth looms Ben Nevis himself.

Now we can see Dunollie above the entrance to Oban Bay. Dunstaffnage is hidden near the cocked ears of Connel Bridge. Out of Dunstaffnage, in May 1493, sailed a little fleet very like Columbus's ships then discovering their New World. This fleet had made its own perilous passage into a world new to most of its men, from Leith around Cape Wrath to bring a king to the hems of his realm. *Christopher, Margaret* and *James* with the Lion ramping at the masthead, Admiral Wood's *Flower* and *Yellow Caravel*, Vice Admiral Barton's *Lyon* and the pinnace *Jenny Pirwin*, they danced over the waves with painted sails.

The mother of King James IV was a Danish-Norwegian princess. In his twenty-first year the salt in his blood stirred him to high adventure.

King James had all the Stewart enthusiasm for learning, with a Renaissance breadth of interests. Art, architecture, music, science, poetry, even manpowered flight, engaged his energies. Soon he would ordain that every freeholder must send at least one son to university. He spoke (according to the Spanish Ambassador) "Latin very well, French, German, Flemish, Italian and Spanish", and, more to the point in his present venture, "the language of the savages who live in some parts of Scotland and the islands". And with all his learning he cherished one ambition, to sail as Admiral of a last crusade against the Turk.

That romantic streak inspired the western voyage. His Gaelic subjects loved glory as he did; he would inspire them with his own zeal and lead them to help him raise Scotland as the Sword of God. He offered friendship for loyalty, learning to match their heritage of myth, chivalric titles to feed their dreams. His new approach was doomed to founder on one basic misapprehension; he saw the Gael as a creature of the mists, dweller in a "twilight" that never was, instead of a hard-headed political animal; and he failed to grasp the essence of the clan system.

For centuries his ancestors had tried to feudalise the west into a recognisable pattern. There had been some progress – chiefs appeared at

Court, castles passed by royal gift, new men, already indoctrinated, were imported – MacNaughtons from Tayside, and others – not enough to leaven the whole. Alien tenure by charter and father-to-son succession were not merely unacceptable, they were meaningless.

The land owned its inhabitants, all, of whatever lineage or status. King James should know that, they could recite his descent though his Court bards might be ignorant of it. Whatever their kinships, their loyalty was first and foremost to the ground beneath their feet. Even Lords of the Isles faced election and summary dismissal for failure. However grand his state, the greatest chief was no more than chosen spokesman and guardian.

The forerunners of the Stewarts themselves, and of all the royal councillors, had set their seals to the 1320 Declaration of Arbroath to inform the Pope, six years after Bannockburn, that Robert Bruce himself was no more than their elected servant:

> *Sed etiam iste Robertus* – yet even that same Robert, should he desert our common cause, would we cast out as the enemy of us all, and choose another king to defend us.

James IV, descendant of Robert and proudly signing himself *Jacobus Seneschallus*, the Steward, knew himself first among equals. His historian John Major wrote that "a king has not the same possession of his kingdom that you have of your coat...it is the free people that first give power to the king..." But feudal notions lingered, despite the lost idealism of the *Morte d'Arthur* and the relegation of the *verray parfit gentil knight* into romantic literature, young James had sailed with chivalric ideals implanted in his mind.

The old Lord of the Isles was beyond redemption, caught in secret treaty with England (for which he lost his earldom of Ross), trounced by his own bastard son at the Bloody Bay off Mull (which disgusted his followers), and again revealed to be "treasonably stuffing Castle Sween with men and munitions of war". He must go, but his younger sub-chiefs were worth winning, such men as Alexander of Loch Alsh, John MacIain of Ardnamurchan, Soldier John of Islay.

They came to the King, and went home with knighthoods and

charters. In theory they had surrendered their lands and received them again with honour, and it was for them to explain their new distinctions to their followers.

Reality broke slowly. It was well enough that the King recognised the clan's worth through its leader; possibly nobody explained that a feudal knight's loyalty lay only to his overlord. In July 1494, after a year spent among the isles, the fleet sailed down Kintyre from Tarbert and put a royal garrison into Dunaverty. That was too much for the Kintyre MacDonalds who summoned Soldier John; before the royal ships were out of sight he hanged the King's castellan from the walls. John's own cousin, Ardnamurchan, delivered him and four of his sons to royal justice; their execution sent a shudder through the west.

The fleet wintered in the Clyde, returning in spring to Mingary. James's mood had changed. He had tried friendship, but to succeed he must soften these barbarians. A hard year on shipboard gave him the idea of raising local living standards. He summoned merchants, and with the very modern thought of introducing industry into backward lands, so barren to Lowland eyes, he fetched a prospector, a "cole man", from Dunbarton – who duly discovered coal at Machrihanish. He also added a tower, and guns, to Tarbert Castle and built a new castle at Lochhead, where Campbeltown now stands; it was not all to depend on improved commerce. Then he rode home to attend to the manifold business of his kingdom, leaving the fleet on station.

In 1497 one of his best new knights, Alexander of Loch Alsh, visited Colonsay on the King's business, raising levies against a north-country MacKenzie rising. A surviving son of Soldier John, with Ardnamurchan himself, murdered the King's man within Oronsay Priory, for trespass upon Islay's preserves. King James returned swiftly and within a year had revoked all charters, ordering the second Earl of Argyll, his Chancellor, to carve the former Lordship into parcels to be let on short lease to reliable tenants, excepting only Islay itself and Kintyre.

Argyll knew his way through that jungle, had marriage ties with many local leaders, readily found trusty tenants of his own people. He was never to complete the task and before it was well begun the Lordship had a new claimant.

Argyll's sister had married Angus MacDonald, the victor of Bloody Bay. Atholl and Argyll were jointly charged to restore peace and Atholl captured Angus's wife and gave her into her brother's keeping. Whether as refugee or prisoner, Argyll sent her to Innis Chonnaill on Loch Awe, where her son Donald *Dubh* (which means both *Dark* and *Luckless*) was born and spent his first twenty years. In the twenty-first the Glencoe MacDonalds spirited him to Harris for acclaim as Lord of the Isles.

The roll-call of his supporters reads like a tartan catalogue – MacLeod of Harris and of Duart, Cameron of Lochiel, MacNeill of Barra, MacQuarrie of Ulva, MacDonalds of every stripe. James, making the same blunder as Magnus Barefoot, had cut off the dragon's head and sown dragon's teeth. From 1502 until 1506 there was war throughout the Isles; armed with 'gun stanes' and German gunners, the fleet bombarded rebel castles, even Cairnburgh Mór –no mean feat in the wild seas off Mull.

At last Lewis and Harris fell and Donald was captured. Long afterwards he escaped for two last years of warfare and a treaty with Henry VIII of England, but James IV never saw that final threat.

He still loved the sea. We hear nothing of Scottish navies, by contrast with English, but in 1511 James launched the biggest ship in Europe, the *Great Michael*, bristling with "very great and costly artillery – six cannons on every side, three great basails and three hundred shot of small artillery, myand and battert-falcon and quarter-falcon, slings, pestilent serpetens and double-dogs, with hagtor and culvering, cross-bows and hand-bows". This dreadnought set off an arms race culminating in England's *Great Harry*; *Michael* made only one unhappy voyage. James, balancing obligations to England against French appeals to the Auld Alliance, ordered his fleet to the French coast. The Earl of Arran, for personal reasons, steered instead towards Ireland. The ships came back as soon as old Sir Andrew Wood reached them, but the harm was done, England had her *casus belli*, Flodden was only a month away.

While the sun shines it is best to forget *The Flowers o' the Forest* and think of a young king walking his decks under bright bunting. He was not wholly mistaken in his offers of friendship, and came close to success. His failure stemmed from ignorance; he and his officials would never believe the 'savages' had different laws. James could not echo Robert I's "I must be with my own", for he never knew what bonds united lands, people and chiefs on the seaboard of his ancestors' earliest roots. He did begin to see the pattern of life in territory linked only by uniting seas; it would be well if modern administrators learned as much.

As we turn under Dunollie a mast glides beyond Kerrera. Almost we expect the Lion to break at the masthead and sails to unfurl at the call of silver whistles; instead a yellow funnel and white topworks reveal a Northern Lights relief-ship setting out. Around the bay, where Boswell gratefully discovered a "tolerable Inn", are tourist-oriented businesses and a railway carrying the lifeblood of the southern isles. Our trainees had better take more notes; past the yacht anchorage they will see a quay packed with fishing-craft. Let their crews have the last word; they know where we have been, they can judge the seamanship that brought *Christopher* to unmarked anchorages and steadied *Flower's* hull off the Treshnish. Winter and summer they sail these highways, and know what waits for little ships.

The Three Brothers

Thon night the three put the sails tie her,
cheerily, heidin home from Ayrshir.
A gale o sutherly wund came on them
By the Cumbrae light, but they werena carein.

Oot thonder by Garroch Heid she trevellt,
runnin lik smok; an' her daicks streamin.
When the rip was risein roond her shoothers,
seas that would swalla, she didna heed them.

West she trampt, an' the white ridges
like bauchkans oot o the night came breengein
against her quarter. Slack they werena
thon night, but the night had a sore endin.

It wasna the wave that the wund wakent,
a steep-faced sea brekkin aboard her,
or a white lump shaken over her shoothers,
that fillt her so that she sank below them.

Ootside o Laggan Heid it struck her
doon from the home hills came boondin
a living squaal that whupt the watter.
It raxed her sail, an' over it threw her.

To their folk's house came the hand o somethin,
through the dark tie the door, an' clasht upon it
three times. At thon uncanny knockin
they couldna speak for the thoughts that were in them.

Their eyes stood in their heid, starein,
an' they wisht they couldna hear the howlin
that the wund made, or the soond o the brekkers
doon on the shore. But aye it was louder.

They gazet in the fire wi gash faces,
an' never talked, for they couldna speak it.
They werena for lyin doon or sleepin,
an' they darena say for why they werena.

Afore the brekk o day in the moarning,
when it wasna derk an' it wasna dawnin,
from the rocks on the rudh' they heard a cryin,
a *céinteach's* keenin. They kent their story.

They kent what yon sore cry was sayin,
an' whose lair was laid on the wrack an' seaweed,
an' they sat there wi the day brekkin,
grey face on the men an' the wommen greetin.

George Campbell Hay, from Wind on Loch Fyne, *Oliver & Boyd, 1948*

15

The Bishop and the Book

EVERY SEASON of the year wears its own livery, from the snowdrops and celandines of spring to midsummer roses and skyblue speedwell. Autumn is heralded by yellow vetches, tall thistles, dark knapweed, and settles into its last calm warmth in a blaze of purple and gold. The October air, misty with bonfire smoke, filters hazy sunshine over the stubbles as the trees begin to glow – gilded birches, red-gold beech, coppery oak, a flame of rowan sparked with scarlet berries. The ash trees are spires of citron tinged with green, a rare sweet chestnut bears its red turned up with silver. The hillside brackens turn bronze among the rocks.

The thin rings of lichen on castle walls are as bright as a shower of coins, largesse scattered from the battlements to knights ahorseback in the orchard where golden-rod and willowherb stand like lances and plumes.

In the valley that runs north from Kilmartin to split at Eurach into two narrow passes, there rises on the western slope the ruin of Carnasserie. From the road, its gables stark above the trees, it might be just one more broken shell from the bad old days; but walk up the rough track under chestnuts and ashes, climb the steep path from the wicket gate and walk sunwise round the garden side. A charming façade looks down, with a string-course of fine masonwork dancing up the wall and the ghost of an oriel window high above. This is no grim coastal tower but a minor Renaissance palace, built by master craftsmen for clients of discernment.

The entrance is on the north side, in the angle of the staircase tower, under a panel bearing the arms of Argyll *per pale* with Scotland, to mark the fifth Earl's marriage to a natural daughter of James V; beneath the shield, a delicate compliment in scholarly Gaelic reads 'God be with O'Duine' in reference to the legendary Campbell descent from Fionn's Diarmaid.

The Campbells were lords of the castle, but entrusted it to hereditary constables named Carswell. There was something here before the present building, perhaps a motte on the nearby rock, and one can see that the east wing of the castle has been partly remodelled – probably an attempt to make the place habitable after a brief and bloody siege in 1685. Inside, notwithstanding, in details of door and stair and fireplaces, one still sees the fashions of James V, with echoes of Stirling and Falkland.

Three little Carswells were born here in the 1520s, Malcolm to succeed his father as Constable, John and Donald to make their own way in the world. John is often credited with the building (he is entitled to claim the entrance panel), but his life held little leisure and scant funds for elegancies.

The brothers would have their first schooling from the priest of Kilmartin, with the neighbour children, and access to a splendid library of Gaelic books collected by the MacLachlans of Craiganterve, a famously learned family (chiefly physicians) who lived close by. John and Donald went to university around the age of fifteen, according to the custom of the time; John entered at St Salvador's College of St Andrews in 1540, and determinated as Bachelor of Arts in 1542. In 1544 *Johannes Corswell, pauper* is licentiated MA. That *pauper* need not mean he was penniless, merely that he did not immediately pay his fee; but the family was of no great wealth, and John may well have carried half a term's supply of oatmeal as he went up Loch Awe to the drovers' way through Glen Dochart and the Roman road across Strathearn.

At half term (still 'Meal Monday' in Scots universities), he brought his Greek and Latin learning back to a Gaelic-speaking home where old tales were remembered and parchments in the Irish script were reverently handled, poems or heroic legends or lives of saints. But the student body of St Andrews was stirred by new currents and preferred modern politics to bygones; John was no exception. He may even – though there are doubts – have been involved in the murder of Cardinal Beaton in 1546; he vanished for two years thereafter.

He reappears in Argyll. It has been suggested that he joined the Benedictine Order in Iona, but I know of no evidence; even there, the monastic life was ending. He did enter the priesthood and in 1555 became Rector of Kilmartin, with the care also of Kilbride – still lifting slender lancets on the green hillside of Rhudil – and little Kilmochummaig beside Crinan. To these he added distant St Blane's in Bute. Such pluralism marks the Church's hopeless understaffing at parish level throughout Scotland;

Gaelic-speaking priests were rare indeed.

Undoubtedly he was collecting appointments. He became Chancellor of Stirling's Chapel Royal, which brought him into the inner circle around the Queen Regent, James V's widow Mary of Guise, who ruled on behalf of her young daughter (in France, and still too young to marry the Dauphin, the future François II). In that ring of intrigue, Argyll led the opposition to the Regent and Carswell was his protegé; but John Carswell had more direct links with the reforming movement.

His brother Donald had gone up to St Leonard's College in 1554, and St Leonard's was a hotbed. Its militant students sang inflammatory ballads and marched to disrupt religious processions; St Andrews gave the Reformers their protomartyr in George Wishart, Knox's master. John Knox himself returned to Scotland in 1555, his sufferings as a French galley slave and his comfortable chaplaincy to Edward VI of England both put behind him, but the final explosion was delayed until 1559.

The Regent outlawed some reformers; by May Knox was preparing a riposte. In July Henry II of France died and the Queen of Scots became Queen Consort of France. French troops came to support the Regent (the French long-term policy envisaging Scotland as a new French province); Argyll found himself facing defeat. Briefly it seemed the Old Religion had triumphed, but within a year the Regent was dead and the French forces withdrew. The Scots Parliament promptly abolished the old forms of religion.

What did they really intend? Reformation had reached them directly from Europe; though some religious houses were sacked, there was no wholesale destruction on the English pattern. Some reform was long overdue; bygone royal patronage had steered the Church's wealth into the hands of bishops and monasteries, and through time much of that wealth had fallen into the keeping of lay Commendators. There was little left to restore country churches or support parish clergy, many of whom existed in near destitution. Many who accepted the need for reform hoped to achieve it without wrecking the whole framework.

A moderate reform is of all things the hardest; once the floodgates open, the tide sweeps all before it, Carswell, basically a moderate man, well knew the plight of Highland parishes. By 1560 he had joined the new Kirk (with many other priests and religious), and was sharing in its optimistic plans.

The keystone was a huge expansion of education, giving everyone power to read the bibles to be provided for every household in the land. The planners expected to handle vast funds, all church revenues whoever had enjoyed them hitherto; tenfold greater than the Queen's patrimony, these would also pay all the ministers needed to expound the Word. Of course such ambitious schemes needed careful management, of course the old order was finished – no more bishops, no more dioceses; but with the country divided into 'districts', each with its 'superintendent', an impartial observer might wonder how much had changed.

Carswell found himself Superintendent of Argyll and the Isles. His authority stretched – and 'stretched' is the word – from Lewis to Kintyre, St Kilda to Rannoch. Even if he set out instantly to tour his territory, he can barely have seen half of it before the young Queen reached Scotland.

Mary arrived in August 1561, in the dazzling beauty of *deuil blanc*, the white mourning of royalty; François II had died a year before. Six feet tall, nineteen years old, she could scarcely remember her home ground. Half her countrymen fell in love with her on sight – half still cherish a romantic dream of her. The reformers were moved to hope they could save her from error; John Knox found in her "some inchantment whereby men are bewitched". Her first act was to forbid interference with "the form of worship public and universally standing". If only it hadn't been a phenomenally wet summer, things might have got off to a good start; but Mary took Edinburgh in loathing, and its citizens blamed her for the rain.

There was far more give and take in the debates between Mary and Knox than legend admits. She kept her own devotion to the old order, but it was she who summoned Knox to return again and again, and she was well able to sustain her side of the argument. The worst blow to Reform came not from Mary but from her Parliament, which assigned two thirds of church revenues to provide for former incumbents and aged religious, and split the remainder between Crown and Kirk.

It was enough to cripple the education proposals, and leave superintendents and parish ministers struggling in poverty. In Carswell's area income had been wholly insufficient before the upheaval; now he had to work with one sixth of that, if he could get it. He wrote to a friend:

> Thus stands the matter in this country; if we crave our stipends,
> and remit them not as the heritors' pleasure, then is our preaching
> unprofitable; yet if we remit them, the travail cannot be sustained
> for fault of sustentation, though we became beggars.

There were four religious houses for men, and one for women, draining funds from his territory. In Iona, Benedictine monks and Augustinian nuns survived to the end of the century, when they became pensioners of the MacLeans of Duart in exchange for lands (many granted, long before, by the Duart family). The nuns were in many cases the formidable maiden aunts of Duart and his fellow landowners; Iona was their chosen retirement home. Cistercian Saddell had already closed down, its last two brethren living in lodgings. Ardchattan had a lay prior supporting his growing family on its farms; on Oronsay the Augustinian Priory was ruinous and all the little churches in Islay and Jura, once served by its Canons, were empty and dark. Here and there a prayer was remembered, a candle lit, but no preachers came to expound the carvings on the great crosses, to grant absolution or conduct marriages.

Strange customs filled the vacuum. Parents anxious to protect a newborn child from the Little People laid cold iron in birth-bed and cradle. They sent a young girl, barefoot and with hair unbound, to fetch water from some spring where passed the living and the dead, going and returning in careful silence, a silver coin glinting in the bowl. The baby's father would make a cross of salt on the water, and name and bless the baby, making it safe from exchange with a wizened changeling.

It is hardly surprising that Carswell accepted the Queen's appointment as titular bishop of his superintendency; there were dedicated rents and funds that he could not otherwise touch. The appointment brought only trouble: the General Assembly rebuked him; Gaelic verses lampooned him for a great greedy heron; and he could obtain only a fraction of the see's revenue. Frustrated and disheartened, he went home to embark on the great work of his life.

No book in any Celtic language had yet been printed (the Welsh Bible ran Carswell close); no fount of type had even been devised. Yet, within two years of its publication in Scots, Carswell put Knox's *Book of Common Order* into Gaelic and saw it through the press. He used everyday speech, not classic forms, with this apology: "If any learned man finds fault with this writing, let him excuse me, for I never acquired any knowledge of the Gaelic except as any man of the people."

If you go through the kitchen and cellars of Carnasserie, and up the narrow stair to the parlour off the Great Hall, you are in the room where the work was done. The sun streams through the big window as it streamed when John sat by the hearth, a log fire gently smouldering and the scent of flowers drifting in. There would be woven wall hangings, scented herbs on the flagstones, a carved chair, a stool or two, a bookshelf (but no such thing as a Gaelic dictionary), a travelworn cloak thrown across a chest.

There he sits. Through the open window-panel comes a robin's autumn song. He lays down his quill; enough of printer's blunders for one day. His eye falls on the leather bindings of books he has loved; he sighs. He ought not to keep them, he cannot bring himself to destroy them. He did try to condemn them – he turns to his Introduction:

> Some of the literature of the Gaels of Alba and Erin is written in manuscripts of poets and bards, and great is the sin of those who prefer vain lying tales of the People of the goddess Danu, or Milesian heroes and Fionn mac Coull and his Féinn, and many others I shall not name, to the faithful. Word of God and the perfect way of truth.

He must rest from poring over proofs; he climbs the stair to the wall-head. There, gazing down the glen in the golden haze, down to the church where his forebears rest, he need not let his eyes stray to the relics of heathendom all around on hillside and valley, need not recall vain lying tales of long ago, heard at the hearthside with his brothers. He can think instead of how to find a competent lay-reader for Kintyre, or to persuade one of the elderly Iona Benedictines to open a school in Mull. Brother Malcolm, now, he has a way with children – and what a memory too; he told me one Chuchullain story that even my mother hadn't known...

"It won't do; you have finished with all such foolishness. Down you go, decide how to answer the letter from Edinburgh, get those proofs packed off. But Lord, Lord, the beauty of Thy earth!"

Inveraray, May 1563

Queen Marie rade doun by Cowal,
At Creggan Ferry the boats were braw;
In the door o the auld gray tower of Aora
Sister-countess loutit ti sister-Queen.

Twa tall sisters dansan thigither,
O mither, see thae bonnie ladies!
I see twa weemen an nae wean atween them,
Breedin an bairnin but breistin name.

What could hairm thae twa bonnie ladies?
See the red heels o them whiles they birl!
Whisht ye, lassie, the twa lang dresses
Are reid wi the bluid o the singan chiel.

O see the bonnie white throat o her turnin,
Twinin, turnin lik the nack o a swan!
Tak ma haun lassie an lead me outbye
Tae greit for the white nack meeting steel.

Lang's the gait a queen maun traivel,
Far frae Aora's Fotheringhay;
Saft in Halyrude sings puir Davie
For sister-countess suppan wi sister-Queen.

Kilberry, 1973

Note

Countess Jane of Argyll was James V's natural daughter. She was at the supper party
in Holyrood, 9 March 1566, when the singer David Rizzio was killed at the Queen's
feet. In 1568 Mary fled to England; she was beheaded in Fotheringhay Castle, on her
cousin Elizabeth of England's orders, in February 1587.

16

Drumly Waters

THE DROUGHT has broken with a vengeance in the flicker of summer lightnings over the sea and thunderclaps volleying between the hills. All night the sky roared down and the house-gutters thrummed; towards morning, the dawn belated by louring rain-clouds, a new note drowned the bass-drumming. The burn began to mutter.

By mid-morning it is the ruling sound, a steady tenor through the dripping and plashing of sodden trees. Honey-coloured at first light, by noon it has reached the deep brown of a full spate and pours over the rock-sluice in a sheet of dark glass, throbbing and pulsing with new freshets from every swollen runnel in the hills. Up on the high tops the clouds shed their burden into blackened deer-moss and bare scree; on the saddles, threads of water glisten like veins of lead, fuse and swell into runlets where the white cotton-grass bows to the ground; between the tussocks the waters muster into streams, streams into burns, burns tumble into the river. It gathers its forces, renews its water-falls, licks dry rocks first with spray and then with foam, then launches the unbroken cataract. *Allt* to *eas*, *eas* to *abhainn*, the waters seek the sea and carry into it their dark fan of peat to stain the grey waves brown.

And there at the rivermouth a flash of silver, a rainbow-arch, and again *there*! something springing faster than the breaking wave and falling back, *there*! The fish are running.

They have waited long for this. The seals have cruised among them feasting; the curved bows of nets have swept them while they waited for water to let them back to the remembered pools where they were spawned. They are home, home from the wide Atlantic. There is something deeply stirring in this blind return year by year of salmon and sea-trout, scenting their way to the sea-loch, the bay, river, feeder-stream, where their lives began. The least sympathetic human must feel a touch of awe. The 'wisest fool in Christendom', King James VI and I, wrote of "the salmon-like instinct to see the place of his birth and breeding", in planning his one journey northward after his accession to the English throne. He had promised to return at not more than three-year intervals, and one visit between 1603 and 1625 is not quite that; but then, he had found he could rule Scotland from London – "I write and it is done" – and he was enjoying unaccustomed ease in his new kingdom.

Behind him lay a harrowing childhood of severities and treachery, of rigorous 'governors' cramming his brain with scholarship and the belief that his mother, the Scarlet Woman in person, had willed his father's murder. He grew up in constant fear of assassination, not without reason. Small wonder that he rejoiced in a respectful court (anyone who had survived Elizabeth's service would find him amazingly flexible) and a church which set him at its head, instead of calling him "God's sillie vassal" to his face. And England was rich, rich enough to meet his wife's debts and his own thwarted extravagance. (That this wealth was in private hands, not in the Exchequer, arose from the old Queen's refusal to summon Parliaments, which alone could agree taxation; squatting on the floor in a red wig, a naked sword hidden among the cushions, she was still Gloriana to her dying breath.)

When they sent for James he left, with scarcely one backward glance, a country riddled with feuds between those who had ruled in his name, manoeuvring for personal gain under a veneer of law. For the commons of Scotland, especially the Gaels, his reign was a time of misery. The governments of his mother, grandfather and great-grandfather had all tried to break down the clan system and bring the Highlands into line, but all they achieved was the sowing of distrust, both of central government and of any leaders who accepted the new order. One example is enough; it comes to mind because of a story I heard while I was fishing in just such a spate as this.

Before James VI left Scotland, he granted the northern half of Jura to MacLean of Duart, leaving the southern half with the Islay MacDonalds. Two Maclean outlaws, to spite their chief, ran a cattle-raid on Jura through Glengarrisdale on its northwest coast. Some Craignish Campbells were at the same game and fell upon the outlaws to seize their loot. One MacLean escaped to fetch reinforcements from Mull; the Campbells sat down to picnic on the battlefield and were caught by MacDonalds following up their cattle. The MacLeans returned in time to attack both parties impartially; the glen was left strewn with men's bones and the blood-feud spread, from atrocity to atrocity, through the Hebrides from Gigha to Barra.

One skull – said to be a MacLean's – has long been enshrined in a rock-cleft in Glengarrisdale. Years ago I was balancing on a spray-drenched rock to cast into a black pool on a small river, when my companion asked if I had seen the Glengarrisdale skull. No, I said, though I had heard of it and had seen other bones exposed under rocks. Well then, Miss Campbell would not have heard of the time the skull was taken away? Just so. His voice assumed the authentic timbre of the *seanachaidh*, the reciter of tales, and I knew I must keep flogging that pool and trust that no fish would be so inconsiderate as to interrupt.

"There was a shepherd at the North End – he wasna a Jura man, his name was MacCorquodale – and here he thought he would make some *money*." (I cannot convey the scorn in that phrase.) "So he took the skull, and he put it in a box, and he sent it to – Miss Campbell will know, would it be a zoo? – aye, just that, it would be a museum. And they paid him for it. And they put it in a glass case. And people would be coming in and looking at it, and it would be jumping up and down and gnashing its teeth at them. And the professors would come in, in the morning, and here they would get it out on the floor. And they would put it back in the case, and in the morning *here* they would get it out on the floor again.

"So there was one wise professor, and he says, 'Boys, that thing's no' canny. Let you take it, and send it back to the man that sent it to us, and tell him to put it back where he got it because it's no' canny'. So they took it, and they put it in a box, and they put it in the post. I'm telling you, Johnny Lindsay would never have gone up the road that night if he had known what was in the box.

"Miss Campbell will know it is late, late, when the post comes to Kinuachrach. Here he comes to the door; 'A parcel for you, MacCorquodale!' 'My, what's this?', and he opens it out, and here's the skull. 'O My,' he says, 'I'll not be going over the hill with you tonight!' But he wasna wanting to be disrespectful, so he took it up the stair to bed with him. And in the middle of the night, *here did the boys no' get it coming doun the stair?*"

The river roars with the voice of an angry ghost in a long-severed Celtic head. There are places that carry their own chill on the brightest day, where, when rain darkens the hills and the mists hang low, one's eye half-catches stealthy movement, one's ear half-hears a soft footfall. Go, if you dare, to Glen Orchy when the spates are out; stand back, for any sake, from the banks, for this is a greedy river that takes a life as readily as it tears away a rock or a birch tree. Stand back, the ground trembling under your feet, and you may yet see, crossing the riven flanks of the braes above the pines, the wraiths of the Children of the Mist, and hear the baying of Glenorchy's black hounds.

This was MacGregor country. They trace their descent from King Gerig or Griogar, grandson of Alpin and nephew of that Kenneth who united Picts and Scots. Their arms display a fallen pine with a crown in its branches; their motto is '*s rìoghail mo dhream*! 'Royal's my race!' From these mountains they preyed upon newer clans with parchment titles to Clan Alpin's hunting-grounds. Out of this wilderness they were hunted – *landless, landless, landless Gregaraich*! cry the pipes – driven to change their name and find surety for good conduct, or else hang. Their women's faces were branded, their children herded into camps run by their enemies. These children could be flogged and branded for trying to escape; a second attempt (or one, if they were over eighteen) was punishable by death.

This bestial business was King James's "parting gift to Scotland", in the words of the editor of the *Privy Council Register*. All chiefs with lands bordering the MacGregor country, from Perthshire to Loch Lomond, took part in the policy, but the experts were Argyll and his kinsman Glenorchy. For many ghastly years the name of MacGregor was proscribed, until at last there remained twelve men who had neither bought safety nor changed their name. They were saved by a dispute between King and Earl over sharing the proceeds of fining those who dared help 'the clan that is nameless by day'.

The wonder is that any of them survived, but they did, much as their language survived the Act of 1616 for establishing schools "that the vulgar Inglische toung be universallie plantit and the Irische language, quilk is ane of the cheif and principall causis of the continewance of barbaritie... abolisheit and removit".

So much for the tongue in which Columba preached. The MacGregors were not the only victims of royal policy; the King in his wisdom had found a Hitlerish solution to several bothersome problems. Much the same treatment was applied to some Borders families. In the identical words used to damn the Gregaraich ("a heinous byke of lawless lymmaris" or wasp's nest of scoundrels) the Outer Isles were offered to the Earl of Huntly on condition he exterminated the natives. A squabble with the Privy Council over the feu-duty payable for this privilege, and the Council's dislike of allowing a Catholic nobleman to extend his territory, saved the Isles.

Southward in Islay Clan Donald was in trouble. Ancient quarrels among its branches spread to embroil MacLeans and MacLeods, and within the branches fathers and sons were at each others' throats. The Bishop of Argyll and the Chancellor, the Earl of Dunfermline, were outsmarting each other to gain Islay for themselves; the castle of Dun Naomhaig ('Dunyveg') was captured, bombarded from the sea, surrendered on treacherous terms, recaptured by MacDonalds. The miserable story drags on through Council decisions and royal letters from Greenwich; the old Earl of Argyll is hounded north to lead his clan, many of them deeply reluctant to serve (the Lady of Dunyveg was Katharine Campbell of Kilberry; she and the children disappeared after the final disaster). The Bishop writes to a friend at Court that to give Islay into Campbell keeping "will be the wreck of my friends, neither can I think it profitable to his Majestie to root out one pestiferous clan and plant one little better".

The work went on among forged papers, *agents provocateur* and perjured testimony. Katharine's husband was betrayed and hanged; his brother Sir James, escaping from long captivity, took to the heather and overran Kintyre even as he put in a bid for his ancestral lands to save the King the cost of "giving employment to the Campbells, who crave ever to fish in drumly waters".

When at last the dust began to settle, Campbell of Calder emerged as crown-tenant in parts of Islay (his name and line accursed in folk-memory), but he was soon suspect. A heroic band of Irish Franciscans entered the Isles to help their fellow Catholics, many of whom could not recall ever setting eyes on either priest or minister. Whole countrysides flocked to the missionaries, who presently claimed Calder himself, a "learned and pertinacious heretic"; he was first contacted by Fr Cornelius Ward, son of a famous Irish bardic line, who made his approach as a harper singing the new laird's praise. The friars voyaged in open boats, camped in caves, existed on shellfish and such scraps of food as their converts could spare – there was famine in the west, among all other ills – while the King laughed heartily to hear that anyone was trying to make Christians of his Gaelic subjects. Sir James MacDonald escaped to Spain, where he was soon joined – in refuge and in religion – by Argyll himself. Once a pillar of the Kirk, the Earl became episcopalian under King James's influence, then in old age made his peace with Rome.

The council had long distrusted Argyll; they suspected his heart was not in the great work of daunting the Isles. "By many it is thought", wrote the Lord Clerk Register, "that if goodwill did second the work of duty, these frequent island employments would not occur so often...how easy it is to have some of these unhallowed people with that unchristian language furnish forth more work for the tinker."

Council and King were estranged from their distant Gaelic subjects and were themselves on a collision course, over James's devotion to episcopacy and his plans for an incorporating union of his two countries. He felt himself, the Most Christian King, no better than a bigamist as long as he ruled two kingdoms; the strength of both countries' opposition surprised him. He sent one English MP to the Tower for intemperate remarks about Scots (a precedent conveniently forgotten); meanwhile his Scottish Privy Council urged him to drop the scheme. But James, who in Kipling's words

Wrote that Monarchs were divine
And left a son who proved they weren't

was not to be told to change his exalted mind. All must learn who was master, and meantime, in his own words, it did nothing but good to "gar ae de'il dang anither" (make one devil beat another).

He never again yielded to his salmon-like instinct, though once tempted by news of an albino deer in the wild country beyond Glen Orchy. A royal huntsman was sent from Windsor Great Park to fetch her within the King's range. The saga of Mr John Scandaver's adventure, seeking the White Hind in the depths of winter, has been worthily told by the late Sir James

Fergusson; it serves to underline the King's divorce from the Celtic world, where a White Doe symbolises the death he feared so greatly.

The sheet of oak-dark water, trembling with its own fury, pours down the rocks in a mass as dense as brown bottle-glass. The spray hanging over it is shot with little rainbows as the sun pierces the lightened clouds. The pool is turning, wheeling, drawing the watcher to surrender to the clotted lumps of peaty froth.

And something moves there, something breaks out, shoots up, hangs fighting in the spray, flashes onward in a twist of silver. He's away on up, he's for the gravel-reaches above, they'll not look at a fly when they're running this hard. The wanderer has returned, as even Clan Alpin was at last permitted to return, "to breathe the kindly air of their home ground".

One last thought occurs, as the rod is taken down and the cast is laid back in the box; how did King James know about the salmon's instinct? Scientists are still studying the phenomenon today. Was it an inspired guess, or another instance of the Stewart bent for science? To toss the fact in as a simile surely implies that his hearers would find it reasonably familiar.

Curiouser and curiouser.

17

Fate and the Hero

UP GLASSARY GLEN on a green May morning go the pipes of war. Behind them lies smoking destruction, not a roof nor a fishing-net left in the heart of Argyll except for that one inn by Stronachullin, where a frightened woman brought a drink of milk to the giant who leads the host. Driven cattle trot groaning past Kilmichael Tryst – no market there, this year of wrath – and the drovers follow, bent under their loot. They missed only one cattlebeast in their sweep around Kilmartin; 'the lowing of the lone cow of Maol-achadh-bheinn' will become a byeword.

It is almost the last great invasion (another, very like, follows in forty years). MacDonalds, MacLeans, MacNeills, march together, as they marched last year with Montrose in his *annus mirabilis* of victories, from Tippermuir to Inveraray, from Inverlochy where the Campbells fell 'like reaped corn' to Auldearn, Alford and Kilsyth. But now Montrose has left the fields of glory, Charles I his master is a prisoner, the giant is giving his followers a last summer's sport on the way home. His name will frighten children for generations; whisht you, or Alasdair MacCholla, *Fear tholladh nan taighean*, the House-burner, will get you.

Sir Alexander MacDonald is huge. At Auldearn he fought alone among the pigsties, shearing pikestaffs from his targe with a sweep of his broadsword. He is ambidextrous, as his father Coll is left-handed (but *Ciotach* can mean 'crafty' too). When his kinsman the Earl of Antrim sought a leader for the Irish royalist troops he was raising, Alasdair drew his blade and cried:

"Here's the best sword-hand in Erin!"

A rival sneered,

"Who then is next best?"

"This!" cried Alasdair, throwing the hilt into his left hand. So he was given charge of the fifteen hundred, and crossing to Morvern added to them the clans that once followed Somerled. From thence he roused Lochaber, and sweeping through the rocky core of Scotland he found and joined the Marquis of Montrose.

Like his ancestor Somerled he is larger than life. He strides through Campbell country like some legendary ogre with a charmed life.

Glassary Glen is green and wide. They go through the village by the church – its Minister presently reports his parish 'desolat of people' – past Kirnan and the tall stone of Lechuary; the Guaire or Gothfruigh commemorated there may be a forebear of Alasdair's own. Up they go between the braes to Loch Leathann, where wild duck scutter out of the reeds at the sounds of their coming.

Near the loch's northern end a small stone building crouches on an island. The island itself, built up to carry it, is a prehistoric lake-dwelling, a crannog, maintained as a refuge. Some countryman has got his family and household gear out to it and now crouches watching, hunting-bow in hand. It's a long shot to the shore, but fury wings his arrow; he sights, draws and lets fly.

The man marching at Alasdair's side throws up an arm and falls dead. A few guns are hastily loaded, a few bows strung, shots splash into the water – but Alasdair has not checked his stride. To their horrified surprise he goes ahead alone, looking neither right nor left – the man must be fey, walking in the grip of fate.

They can only follow, yelling promises to return and exact a deadly vengeance. Downhill they pursue him, past Stroneskar to where Loch Ederline shines in its cup of reeds. And suddenly they find that news of their coming has outrun them.

In the narrow passage along the lochside, men of the district have gathered. They are led – so tradition says – by Zachary Mór MacCallum (who should have been reading divinity at Glasgow, on a Synod of Argyll bursary shortly to be withdrawn). There is room to sweep past, but when has MacDonald refused battle? Loads are shed, plaids thrown aside, the cattle push their way to the rich waterside grasses. Zachary steps forward to challenge Alasdair to single combat.

And why not? It is entirely in character to venture the whole affair on his own sword-luck. The two parties rest on their swords to watch the duel, the Swordsman of the Western World against the small dark man, or alternatively Ogre versus Prince. The MacDonalds are inclined to pity the boy's rash daring, he that should be at his books.

A blade cartwheels in the sunlight. A yell of triumph breaks out, but it breaks from the Kilmartin men. Alasdair stands, bewildered and defenceless, rubbing his numbed arm.

At last he finds his voice, strange and harsh as a tranced man's.

"What place is this?" They tell him *Goc-an-gò*, the False Outlet, long ago the outfall of Loch Awe by way of Eurach.

He is stunned. His old Islay nurse prophesised that if her nurseling ever came to somewhere called *Gocam-gò*, his luck would leave him. Nobody had worried, nobody knew a place named, in the Islay Gaelic, 'look-out-man' or 'spy' – what sort of a name was that?

But Alasdair has broken his lifetime taboo, his *geas*, as heroes of old broke *geasa* by some trivial act.

The hero's fate has come. Nothing now can save the day; *Bundle and Go* is the tune for the pipes as they take the hill road again.

Back past Kilmichael to Loch Gilp, past the Inn of Taigh-an-Droighinn and up the steep flanks of Sliabh Gaoil. There are places up there where the droveroad climbs that ten men could hold against an army, but Alasdair posts no rearguard. Furies pursue him, in fancy and in fact, for that seasoned old campaigner David Leslie, veteran of the Swedish wars, is on his heels. Alasdair speeds on, southward through Tarbert to Rhunahaorine where he packs his men into commandeered boats and sets off for Islay; three hundred must be left behind to make the best of their fate, packing into Dunaverty for a last stand under MacDonald of Sanda. Alasdair has abandoned the mainland.

Old Coll holds the ancestral keep of Dùn Naomhaig. Alasdair joins him briefly before fleeing on to Ireland, where he dies in a petty skirmish. Dùn Naomhaig falls and Coll is hanged from his own ship's mast; Dunaverty falls, and the ministers who have marched with Leslie dabble their shoes in the garrison's blood.

The *geas* has won.

18

The Ill Years

IT SELDOM snows hard on the coast. On crisp mornings one wakes to see a level white band ruled along Jura, and to hear cat-ice crackling under a wheel; you set out on a road lightly rimed, drive past grizzled braes, and at the crest of the pass all Lochfyneside lies gleaming white to the waterline.

Mid-January is when a few fat swan's feathers sail gently down, succeeded by dry tickly specks that thicken into a suffocating cloud. Once in ten years, maybe, the big falls come; powerlines collapse, gates crumple to scrap-iron, a gamekeeper's spaniel snuffles out ewes trapped below whin-bushes. In other years we may have one snowy day, though fifty miles away the ski slopes are thronged.

I came once to Ballachulish from the north, through snow flurries, to find the perfect white diamond of Sgurr na Cíche and its reflection mirrored in Loch Leven's jewelled surface. The sky was black, but the ferrymen (these were pre-Bridge days) reported traffic crossing Rannoch and snowploughs working. Past the disused slate-quarries masked in ice, I reached the turn into the hills.

Whooper swans were paddling in circles, keeping open water on the loch below Ossian's Cave. The black rocks soared, their clefts infilled with white; from Aonach Eagach the big flakes swooped. On the highest corner the Smith's Apron hung like plate glass; blinding whiteness met me – change down again, forget the brakes, follow veering lorry-tracks (trusting he could see the road). A black halfmoon rising suddenly must be the arch of the old bridge.

Here all is white or black, sharp as a moral judgement, no hint of 'maybe'. Ahead lies Rannoch, one whirling yellowish mass into which the tracks vanish under a dance of snowdevils.

Orange eyes glare, dark shapes loom; I pull over cautiously to let the Mountain Rescue convoy through towards the terrible hills; some fool has defied the Old Ones and these men must risk their lives for him. Has there not been enough death here already?

"A savage spot, as holy and enchanted..."; blood-hallowed ground, haunted by an act so dreadful that it cannot be forgotten. We forget easily; Lidice, Belsen, My Lai – what were they? – but the world remembers Glen Coe. All the world knows that here, some bygone time, out of innate vice, Campbells killed MacDonalds. Some people are surprised to learn that there are any MacDonalds still alive. To question the story is vain, to hint at darker truths behind the legend is like spitting into the wind. Let us at least collect some facts; God knows they are bad enough.

Yes, there was a massacre, in February 1692, fit climax to a century of horrors. From the time when the Outer Isles were on offer to those who could depopulate them, through blood-money for MacGregor children's heads, to Episcopalians, Catholics, and Covenanters killing, torturing and suffering martyrdom, men's minds grew numb. Charles II, England's 'Merry Monarch', ruled Scotland's Killing Time.

His heir was his brother; "Jamie, Jamie, nobody is going to kill me to make you King!" But there was nobody else; Jamie became King James VII and II, and the Rising led by Charles's natural son Monmouth, and the ninth Earl of Argyll, ended in disaster.

James's two daughters were his heirs, until the birth of his son in 1688 revived Protestant fears (Table 6, p.217).

The English took fright first. James, always his own worst enemy, declared his intention to restore normal liberties to all religious minorities including his fellow-Catholics. Three generations had died opposing toleration; England sent envoys to the Princess Mary's husband, the staunchly Calvinist William of Orange, and his envoys in turn entered Scotland.

To the Scots, William was the son of a Stuart princess and the husband of another; many Scotsmen served in his armies. The English saw him rather as a referee coming to ensure fair play. The Scottish Estates, meeting in convocation (Parliament could not meet without a royal command), showed a last flicker of tradition, declaring that James had forfeited his throne (England said he had abdicated), and offering a joint contract to William and Mary II. They did not know their Dutchman.

William's lifework was to defeat France, all else was incidental. With

Britain's help he could win; with Britain neutral he could fight on; with Britain aligned by James beside his enemy, he might be overwhelmed. A cold, secret, calculating man, he trod towards the thrones without undue concern for details.

Half Scotland opposed him; his army was routed at Killiecrankie by the clans, but their leader Dundee was killed and his forces could be penned into the hills behind a line of garrisons – though these were expensive diversions of manpower.

In August 1691 the Campbell Earl of Breadalbane brought Highland leaders to Achallader in Rannoch, to consider submission. He had money available for *douceurs* (although it proved curiously difficult to account for), and he was empowered to offer indemnity for all bygone rebellion provided the chiefs swore loyalty to the new regime by next New Year's Day. Messengers were permitted to travel to the court-in-exile at St Germain to obtain King James's leave to change allegiance. Dilatory as usual, James replied on 12 December; his messenger struggled exhausted to Dunkeld by 21st, pleading for an extended deadline. The Scottish Privy Council felt itself unable to grant it; besides, some of them had other plans.

There is an ancient belief that good rulers bring good seasons. The joint reign of William and Mary coincided with seven years of rain and hunger. 'King William's Ill Years' became proverbial (nobody blamed poor Mary, who doted on her husband). Crops failed, cattle died, people starved, especially those who had troops quartered on them.

Instead of a delay, William ordered a general assault on all who failed "to take the benefit of our gracious indemnity", adding that he hoped "not to be burdened with the expense of prisoners". An English nobleman chancing to hear this last clause, the plan was slightly amended – one clan should die to encourage the rest. The Scottish Secretary, Sir John Dalrymple, should select the example.

Dalrymple had given the matter some thought, telling the military governor of Inverlochy that "the winter is the only season in which we are sure the Highlanders cannot escape... This is the proper season to maul them, in the long cold nights."

William said he hoped his commanders "would show no more zeal against the Highlanders after their submission than they have ever formerly done when these were in open rebellion." Thus the stage was set.

Dalrymple first considered MacDonald of Keppoch, but something unknown diverted him; "Argyle tells me that Glencoe has not taken the oath, at which I rejoice. It is a great work of charity to be exact in rooting out that damnable sect."

King James's letter reached his supporters at Glengarry, and Lochiel went immediately to Inveraray, making oath before the Sheriff on 31 December. The chief of the Glen Coe MacIains, a division of Clan Donald displaced from Ardnamurchan by Campbells, was old, and balked at crossing Rannoch. Instead he went to Inverlochy. Colonel Hill, the Governor, was not empowered to administer the oath, but gave MacIain a letter acknowledging his good intentions. This time the Moor was passable, and MacIain reached Inveraray on 1 January. The Sheriff's express to the Council was later expunged from official records.

On 16 January William despatched a brief document signed and countersigned by himself alone:

> WILLIAM R. As for MacIan of Glencoe and that tribe, if they can well be distinguished from the rest of the Highlanders, it will be proper for public justice to extirpate that set of thieves. W.R.

MacIain came home content to have saved his people, glad the troops quartered in the glen knew of his efforts. Their captain was Robert Campbell of Glenlyon, related both to the MacIains and to Breadalbane. Apologists for Glenlyon suggest he was vulnerable to pressure 'because of personal debts to Breadalbane'; scarcely any Highland landed family was solvent, after penalties incurred in recent troubles. Breadalbane himself was in trouble over the Achallader funds.

The pressures on Robert were more probably those felt by most soldiers in revolutionary times; his immediate superior, Major Duncanson, soon set them out. Further, Robert was probably the kind of junior officer who never wins promotion, an executant without ability to take independent decisions. Every revolution is full of them, might well fail without them.

It was a pity that King William did not see the letter Major Duncanson wrote to Robert from Ballachulish on 12 February, shortly before marching into the snowstorm; it was endorsed, for good measure, "By the King's especiall command", and he would have approved:

> Sir: you are hereby ordered to fall upon the rebels, the MacDonalds of Glencoe, and put all to the sword under (the age of) seventy. You are to have special care that the old fox and his sons do upon no account escape your hands. You are to secure all avenues, that no man escape. This you are to putt into execution att five o'clock in the morning precisely, and by that time, or very shortly after it, I'll strive to be att you with a stronger party... See that this be putt in execution without feud or favour, else you may expect to be treated as not true to the King's government, nor a man fitt to carry a commission in the King's service. Expecting you will not fail in the fulfilling hereof as you love yourself, I subscribe these with my hand. – Robert Duncanson.

That left little doubt.

The Glencoe company, and Duncanson's stronger party, belonged to Argyll's Regiment. The belief that 'they were all Campbells' springs from ignorance of the Army structure, which named every regiment after whoever raised or commanded it. Its Colonel exerted patronage, but promotion in King William's army, as in Queen Victoria's, came by purchase; the rank-and-file might be volunteers, tenants' sons (recruits counted in lieu of purchase money), drifters, or jail-sweepings.

Glenlyon's men were spread around the township as he read his letter. What now? He can kill himself rather than obey – that dooms his wife and children, and cannot save the MacIains; his Lowland subalterns will carry out the orders. Could he somehow warn his hosts? Should he simply let blame fall where it should, on his seniors? Let those who judge war-crimes assess this case; it is not for armchair historians three centuries late.

A Berwick or a Marlborough might have sent his juniors to cut trail towards Duncanson, and himself led the MacIains through one or another snow-choked pass. Next day the soldiers rounded up "900 cattle, 200 horses, numberless herds of sheep and goats" – such a drove could have trampled a road, and the troops would have followed on it. If any survivor reached shelter, those who took them in would also be doomed.

It is believed he tried to sound one alert; his piper went through the snowy dusk playing *Women of this glen, take warning!* Those who recognised the tune thought the choice odd, but the piping world loves cryptic gestures; serious messages have been conveyed in the far-sounding music; two of the chief's sons kept watch, and raised the alarm when the troops fell in.

The snow defeated Duncanson, Glenlyon's men had it all to do. The number of victims is disputed; the maximum seems to be 35 men including the chief, two women, and two children. One is too many – though as a 'clan massacre' it pales beside the 200 MacDonalds reportedly suffocated in the Cave of Eigg, a century earlier, by MacLeods. Some 200 MacIains escaped from Glen Coe, floundering through snowy bogs to bring the word to Glen Etive, Achallader, Corrour.

The shockwave swept Scotland. Breadalbane revealed nothing, but Argyll had no doubts; he would never escape the stain of Secretary Dalrymple's 'work of charity'. Argyll's people gave what help they could, settling survivors as far away as Knapdale. The shock did not awaken rebellion, but jangled through the links between clans and played some part in future distrust of aliens, revived loyalties to the Stuarts, reluctance to take any side at all.

The story broke over London in a shower of anti-government handbills screaming *News from the North!* before official returns even reached Whitehall. Obviously things had misfired. The Opposition demanded an Inquiry, as did the Queen, little realising where the guilt lay. (Mercifully she died before the first well-massaged Preliminary Report appeared.) Official propagandists encouraged the view that northern barbarians had run true to form, one pestiferous clan against another. Argyll's Regiment went to the Flanders front.

Nothing can wipe the bloodstains off the rocks, no thaw melts the dead-chill of Glen Coe. It returns and returns, the atrocity and its propaganda, but let us make an end soon. Surely we who know of Lidice and all the other horrors of our time – or can learn of them – can find some bitter pity for the heirs of Cain.

John o'Lorn

My plaid is on my shoulder, and my boat is on the shore,
And it's all by wi' auld days and you;
Here's a health and here's a heartbreak, for it's hame my dear no more,
To the green glens, the fine bens we knew!

It was for the sake o'glory, but wae upon the wars
That brought my father's son to sic a day!
I'd rather be a craven, wi' nor name nor fame nor scars
Than turn an exile's heel on Moidart Bay.

You, in the day-time, you'll be here, and in the mirk,
Wi' the kind heart, the open hand, and free,
When far awa' in foreign France, in toun, or camp, or kirk,
I'll be wondering if you keep a thought for me.

But nevermore the heather nor the bracken at my knee!
I'm poor John o'Lorn, a broken man,
For an auld Hielan' story, I must sail the singing sea,
A chief without a castle or a clan.

My plaid is on my shoulder, and my boat is on the shore,
It's all by wi' auld days and you,
Here's a health, and here's a heartbreak, for it's hame my dear no more
To the green glens, the fine bens we knew.

Neil Munro

Note
This version, written into my autograph book by the poet himself at Ford Loch Awe
in 1928, differs slightly from printed texts.

19

An Older Law

THE HOUSE of Inverawe stood with its back to Cruachan Beann and its door wide to the sunlight. Down by the river the reapers whetted their scythes and the women went stooping as they bound the sheaves. Beyond them sparkled Loch Etive, blue and windless.

The laird had been working in the field; his wife and the children were there yet, carrying round the scones and the jugs of oatmeal-bree to lay the dust of harvest. He stood in his doorway and looked over the golden valley.

As he turned, a movement upriver caught his eye; a moment later and he would have missed it. Bushes were stirring – had a heifer louped the dyke? No, he could see now, no heifer but a man, running past the fallow-field, jumping the ditch – a man in a hurry, a man unknown. He started towards him.

The runner, gaining open ground, put on a spurt that brought him to the house. Before Duncan could begin to speak, the stranger had ducked past him.

Duncan followed, not a little astonished. The fellow was on his knees by the hearthstone, bent double and fighting for breath, one hand gripping the butt of a smouldering log in the little fire of a summer's day.

"You're in fair haste, friend – what ails you?"

Half his mind still dwelt on harvest-time; in the other shadowy half where memory lives, some touch of older things began to prickle.

The man coughed and gasped, swung round, and was suddenly and shockingly grovelling at Duncan's feet.

"Shelter...hide me...they'll get me...they're no' far ahint!"

"Your hand on my hearth, I'll not deny you refuge. Can you tell me your need? Nay, I'll not ask a name, never fear."

Out of those shadows, the one word *Gregarach*. But that evil was past, nobody hunted MacGregors these days. The torn tartan told him nothing – a faded greyish thing that once had a stripe in it. Some wretch in flight from

135

an ale-house brawl, and pursued by fellow-rogues? The face at knee-level, distorted in terror, was now disgustingly streaked with tears.

"Get up for shame, man! Take a grip of yourself and come through to the kitchen for a bite of food."

"No, no, hiding...into hiding...they're at my back...I got above them on the braes of Brander, but there's five in it, and two of them with guns."

Hell, this is more than a thieves' quarrel, I'll need to learn more. But his mind was flooded with thoughts of the games he'd played with his foster-brother and the tales they used to hear – how men of old took sanctuary at a house-fire and how their hosts would die to protect them even from a friend. Neil and he had often acted out those tales, and in the Year Fifteen there had been kinsmen of his own who owed their lives to just such ancient loyalties. He could not deny his own past simply because a man's weeping sickened him.

"Hold up and come on. Here, take the cheese, and this loaf – you'll have a knife."

The creature shuddered.

All right, we'll do the thing properly; Neil will grin when I tell him this later. He led his man across the yard, out of sight of harvesters and those sharp-eyed boys of his. Down through the little wood, across the burn in the gully, up the flank of Cruachan by the way he and Neil always went. There was a clump of birches, and behind them an ivy-covered rock. It was the place his father had shown Neil and himself, the old secret place that he'd show his own sons when they were old enough, though God forbid they should need the knowledge. He pulled aside the ivy-tod:

"In with you. It's roomy, and dry, and a wee trickle of spring-water in the angle. You're safe now for your three nights."

He cut short the babble of thanks and went quickly downhill. Three nights' safety – a fireside story come to life; he shook his head. He'd take a hard look at the hunters if they ever showed up, and if they were the sort he expected he'd whistle up some of the men and hale them off to justice.

It was much later, when his wife had brought little Janet home weary from running and shouting among the stooks, that he heard steps coming to the door. He went out ready to put the hard word on whoever stood there, but the man whose hand was raised to the tirling-pin was a cousin of his own.

"Duncan! Thank God you're at home – did you see a stranger go down the pass? Duncan – how am I to tell you – it's Neil…knifed in a damfool silly argument up in Glen Strae…the man broke from us up the hill, we've swept the braes as we came…"

And Jean's voice behind him:

"Neil? O not Neil, not dead, not Neil!"

And Janet beginning to wail because her mother was crying.

The river rushed, an owl hooted above Bonawe, the night was at its darkest. He woke suddenly with a name on his lips: *Neil*. And there was Neil himself, beyond the bed-curtains, not any more the supple boy he'd raced up Cruachan but bent over a mortal wound. He could see it was mortal from the way Neil held himself, even before he saw the blood. He was half out of bed when he remembered the day's work. He cried *Neil*! aloud, and Jean stirred in her sleep and put out her hand to him.

There was plenty to be done, funeral arrangements, messages to kinsmen, to the minister, to the sheriff. He was busy all day long, with ever, at the back of his mind, horrible thoughts of the man in the cave. His word was pledged for three nights – but what if he told the sheriff where to post his men? A man must uphold the law, but he had acted under an older law. Well then, by that older law the blood-feud was his own. If he took a good gun and lay out on the hillside, that fourth morning… He shook himself angrily, angry even to think such a thing, angriest of all with the cowering animal he'd protected. How dared the wretch pick on him, of all men? What use was revenge? It would not bring Neil home. By nightfall he was exhausted.

Neil. A thin shaft of moonlight touched the chair and the wallpress, and between chair and bed-curtain stood the grey silhouette, faint as smoke except where the dreadful other colour spread. He propped himself on his elbow, careful not to waken Jean.

"Neil – you know how it was, you must understand. I promised him, Neil – I couldn't know, how could I? I gave him the hearthword of safety."

The chair shone in the moonlight, the smoky shape had gone. Duncan did not sleep again that night.

The third evening Jean was distressed for him, kept the children quiet, wanted him to drink a hot posset at bedtime. He did not expect to sleep, but he must have slept. A rainy night, no moon, the river roaring.

Stark awake: *Neil.* Again he tried to argue, to explain. *Dear to man is a brother, but the heart's pith the foster-brother*; his dear companion was fading from him, turning into a spiteful menacing ghost that hid all the good memories.

"I tell you, I promised him – I can't go back on my given word, you must know that, you can't expect it. Neil, Neil, speak to me, in the name of Heaven's mercy give me one word of comfort!"

The shadow quivered, and spoke.

"We shall meet, "it said, "at Ticonderoga."

He was on the hill before sunrise. As he climbed he muttered the extraordinary, the unforgettable word. *Taigh* what? The house of *where*?

Under the ivy-tod, a clear footprint pointing outward. The cave was empty.

Eighteen years later Major Duncan Campbell sat by an army campfire in the woods of Lake George. His younger son was in the cluster of junior officers laughing around the blaze. From a little way off came the voices of soldiers and Indian guides; a piper was fingering a jig. The 42nd Regiment of the Line, the Black Watch, was in the field against Montcalm himself.

Now that he was far from Scotland Duncan could speak of past events without undue emotion and join in fireside tellings of ghost-stories with a quiet certainty. The whole regiment knew of his appointed rendezvous, and when one of the Indians let slip their name for the French stronghold before them, the regiment united to keep the fatal word from Inverawe's hearing. The poor fellow, *an duine bochd*, why would we tell him the like of that, and he the fine man that stood to his word in face of the living and the dead?

There had been the usual military miscalculations that dogged all British armies on American soil. Fort Carillon was not the lightly-held outpost Lord Abercromby believed it to be. Redcoat waves broke vainly on its palisades until at last the pipes sang out and the green tartan went forward. Duncan led them up the slope, over the dead to the last stockade and up it. One cry above the tumult, and Inverawe fell back into his son's arms.

It was merely a scratch from a spent bullet, but it sufficed. Days later, in the misery of a field-hospital, he whispered to young Alexander,

"Fort Carillon's not the real name. Neil, too, kept his word and came to meet me there, in the breach of Ticonderoga."

20

A Spring of Poetry

FROM ONICH to Blair Atholl and from Laggan Bridge to Tyndrum, there lies in the heart of Scotland a great lozenge of roadless country. The main road to Inverness curves along its eastern border, the road from Laggan to Spean Bridge forms the north-west side; from Kinlochleven to the Tyndrum crossroads the A82 flanks it, and the way to Killiecrankie by Loch Tummel completes the circuit. One minor road strikes inward from the east, only to fail at Rannoch Station in face of the Moor.

There is a recurrent phrase, a 'run', which is used in every Gaelic tale of flight and pursuit. Hero or villain goes through 'seven bens and seven glens and seven mountain moors', and the simplest way to put flesh on the bones of that statement is to look out over the Black Mount from near Loch Bà.

This is glacier country. The waters lie in ice-holes, the hillsides have been scarped by vast grinding ice-sheets. If you cannot go and see for yourself, look at any contoured map and see how closely the height-lines are packed, how often a placename contains the word *coire*. It means a cauldron, and has entered worldwide mountaineering language to describe a steep-sided hollow with a lakelet in its floor, high up some peak where an icecap sagged towards a passing glacier, and where now the winter snows linger. The word is universal, the reality familiar to those who come into this wilderness 'Munro-bagging', climbing the peaks over 3,000 feet which here abound.

They see the heart of the diamond as no road-user can; they hear the ring-ousels' music and see the eagles soar above the grazing deer. There is, too, another way; it curls along the north-east edge of Argyll into Lochaber and disgracefully, in a country that claims to be tourist-conscious, it is under-used and grossly under-publicised.

The Highland Railway glides up to the thousand-foot contour above Tyndrum, rolls between Beinn Bheag and Beinn Odhar, and sweeps in a giant arc above the marshy watersmeet where Auch Farm stands. In parts it is protected by slatted fences of old sleepers, occasionally by roofed snow-tunnels. The motor-road opposite is marked by huge upright tree trunks; the summer tourists can scarcely credit that these posts are set for the guidance of the snowploughs whose drivers will, with luck, see their tips poking out of white slopes. To cross Rannoch by train, in spring or summer, is to see the big tops patched with snow and blue with racing cloud-shadows, and deer feeding unconcerned beside the line. Here and there in the peat one may glimpse a buried tree stump, a relic of the Black Wood of Caledon whose last survivors toss their red branches by Loch Rannoch and along Glen Falloch – the Scots pines that clothed these hills when man was a newcomer.

Few people live around Rannoch Moor now – signalmen, track-layers, a shepherd or two, a stalker or two – but in green gullies the bracken grows thick around tumbled walls. Men have lived here, alongside the deer, before sheep came to displace them both, and only a man whose life centred on these hills could truly set out their infinite and terrible beauty.

He would need to be a poet; mere recitation of heights and contours is not enough, nor botanical lists nor even the stirring account of a new climbing-traverse.

> 'S e Coir' a'Cheathaich nan aighean siùbhlach,
> An coire rùnach as ùrar fonn,
> Gu lurach, miad-fheurach, mìn-gheal, sùghar,
> Gach lusan flùar bu chùbhraidh leam

The trouble with good poetry is that it is untranslatable; idea and language have fused. Another poet can make the idea his own and restate it, but not in its virginal clarity. Others can only produce the crude outline:

> Corrie of the mists and the restless deer,
> Lovely corrie of the freshest air,
> Pasture of soft and sappy grazings
> Whose scented flowers were dear to me...

One was taught to consider 'nature-poetry' a nineteenth-century discovery to be associated with Wordsworth and his friends; but to be truthful,

141

Wordsworth was a philosophic moralist who used nature-metaphors. Poetry about nature is something else; it has had its place in Gaelic and Welsh literature from the earliest times, alongside the other major themes – love, satire, laments, voyagings, praises. If the proof were still needed that a body of classical verse survived in common circulation within the Highlands, to and beyond the eighteenth century, then one man's work provides that proof. The verse I have just mangled in translation is the opening of *The Misty Corrie* by *Donnchadh Bàn Mac-an-t' Saoir*, Fair Duncan MacIntyre, an unlettered deerstalker.

He has used one of the classical metres of the *filidhean*, requiring a set number of syllables and a rhyme-scheme with internal assonances. The rhymes of Gaelic poetry are between vowels, not consonants, so that those *ù* and *ì* sounds tie the verse together, other stressed vowels playing around them like sunlight on water. The range of vocabulary needed to find such harmonies is worth consideration; so is the knowledge of metrics, pointing to close study of medieval exemplars; so is the underlying observation that echoes, in cascades of imitative sound, the movement of bird and beast.

We are too apt to confuse literature with literacy, as we are to look across such empty landscape as this and call it a wilderness. If one likes to be pedantic one could call a *filidh* illiterate because he was forbidden to use writing. He studied metres and techniques through seven long years of training; how long must a man study who has no tutor but his own gift?

'Fair Duncan of the Songs', as he is lovingly known to this day, was born on 20 March 1724 at the now deserted township of Druimliaghairt in Glenorchy, and died in Edinburgh on 14 May 1814. His wife, Mairi MacIntyre, was daughter of Nicol, keeper of the inn at Inveroran (it was she whom we 'have not seen with Duncan's eyes'). At 21 Duncan was hired to take a local farmer's place in the Hanoverian militia, and set off carrying his hirer's old sword to the civil war of 1745. At the Battle of Falkirk he fled, like most of the Government forces, shedding the sword as he ran. So Demosthenes lost his shield at Chaeronea and Horace at Philippi; like Horace, Duncan got a song out of his loss – a brisk satire on the rusty blade, its craven owner, and the cause for which he had (or hadn't) fought. Tradition claims this *Song to Fletcher's Sword* was Duncan's first; it shows his technical skill already well-grown. It was a fit opening; satire was the master-gift of the old bards. Fletcher refused to pay the agreed fee; Duncan retorted in verse, and the song so pleased Lord Breadalbane that he appointed Duncan his stalker for Ben Dorain.

For twenty years Duncan walked the hills, first from a house near Bad-odhar and later at Dalness. Then well-meaning friends found him an easy billet in the City Guard in Edinburgh, so that he left his beloved hills – although he often returned to walk throughout the Highlands, his wife beside him in her red cloak and he in his kilt and his old foxskin cap.

He was 69 when he enlisted in Breadalbane's Fencibles, during the invasion-scare of 1793, and served with them until they were disbanded in 1799. In 1802 he made his last trek westward, composing a *Last Farewell to Ben Dorain* as he sat on a rock near Auch, too moved to complete the poem. Twelve years later he died, and was laid to rest in Greyfriars churchyard, ten years short of his century.

His verses were first printed in 1768, taken down from his dictation by a Gaelic-speaking minister. The need to rely on transcribers led to editorial meddling over the years; the great *Ben Dorain* was recast during his lifetime, apparently to give it a more 'lively' ending. Fortunately the first edition survives to show the original intention. The reader must always bear in mind that, wherever the composition was formed, it had then to be carried in Duncan's mind, sometimes refreshed by a new insight, sometimes declaimed to a gathering of friends and then partially transferred into their memories, but lost to posterity unless and until a scribe came along to set it down to the best of his ability.

The *Praise of Ben Dorain* would be remarkable enough for its literary skill and its rich vocabulary; to this must be added the bravura flourish of imitating a classical bagpipe composition of approximately sonata form – called in English a 'pibroch' (though this word comes from *piobaireachd*, meaning simply 'pipe-music'). In this treatment a slow theme or 'ground' alternates with progressively more elaborate variations.

The poem depicts the whole mountain-world in a verse-cycle of five hundred and fifty-five lines. They might be described in musical terms as *Largo*, the Mountain and the Hunter; *Andante cantabile*, Hind and Stag; *Allegro pastorale*, the Dawn, *Alla marcia*, Huntsmen and Hounds, and so on; but this hides something of the achievement. Not only does the verse catch the very beat of movement, but the animals are themselves, the hind is all Hind, the dogs are pure Dog, unsentimentalised, material creatures running over a material hillside of shining grass. It would be worth any poet's and any naturalist's while to acquire enough Gaelic at least to grasp an outline of this masterpiece. Fortunately they have been spared even that much effort by a splendid new translation of *The Praise* by the modern Gaelic poet Iain Crichton Smith (and how I wish he would undertake the rest of Duncan's *oeuvre*).

Each new collection of the poetry produced new marvels until the *Last Farewell*:

> *Mo shoraidh leis na frìthean,*
> *O's miòrbhailteach na beannan iad;*
> *Le biolair uaine is fior-uisg,*
> *Deoch uasal, rìomhach, cheanalta...*

("My blessing on the deer-forests, from the marvellous hills of them, with the green cresses and clear springs, gentle rich sweet drink... my thousand blessings for ever on them").

The issue of a city policeman's ditties in a barbarous tongue could not excite the admiration of the Polite World. That world was wholly absorbed in the controversy surrounding the revelation of an older Celtic poetry. In 1760 a young graduate of Edinburgh named James MacPherson produced translations entitled *Fragments of Highland Poetry*. He claimed to have gathered them from oral and manuscript sources. Edinburgh society was torn between doubt and admiration, as it was already torn between a proud adherence to bygone glories and uneasy attempts to appear as English as possible for political success. The *Fragments* were linked to the mystic figure of Ossian, a gaunt wild-bearded survivor from the days of 'Fingal', lingering on earth long enough to dispute with St Patrick (at least an historical personage, though Irish and – whisper it – of The Other Persuasion). Heated debate arose, MacPherson doing nothing to help his cause by declining to produce his manuscripts and by "refining and elevating" his text to an absurd degree. English students of literature were drawn in; a search

144

for 'Ossianic originals' was one motive for Dr Johnson's northern journey. When he returned empty-handed he threw his considerable weight into denouncing MacPherson's work as forgery. Nobody thought of consulting that insignificant policeman, although he had lightly introduced 'Ossianic' heroes into his work:

> *Ged thig Caoilte 's Cuchullain,*
> *'S gach duine de'n t-seors' ud,*
> *Na tha dhaoine 's de dh'eachaibh*
> *Air fasta Righ Deorsa –*

("Though Caoilte came, and Cuchullain, and every man of that sort, with all King George's men and horses," they couldn't find or catch the roe-doe swift as a spark).

'Ossian' MacPherson rose above all adverse criticism, and arranged for his body to lie in Poet's Corner within Westminster Abbey. Born in Ruthven Barracks in 1738 and brought up nearby, he went from Inverness Grammar School to Aberdeen University and thence to Edinburgh – so he can have been no sort of fool. His literary fame got him employment as a government pamphleteer and eventually a seat in Parliament. He left money to publish his 'originals' and a few scraps did appear, but proved of scant value. Despite that, he had many admirers, among them Napoleon Bonaparte who had his bedroom ceiling painted with Ossian and the *Féinn*.

There was no shutting Donnchadh Bàn into a Poets' Corner. His admirers built a little classical rotunda to his memory; it takes the eye on a low hilltop as one goes from Loch Awe towards the big tops he loved; but his abiding monument is Ben Dorain itself, the pure cone hanging over Auch or, from the road to Glencoe, a long serrated ridge which is disconcertingly like the ridge of Yeats's Ben Bulben.

Like a mountain-spring he had loved, the 'pipe-well of Ben Dorain', the Gaelic language had been forced underground, the tongue of boors and heretics, of a dumb and ignorant peasantry. But the speech and its images still coloured the thoughts of other poets, Thomas Campbell for one. Born in Glasgow in July 1777, of a father whose home lay in Glassary and a mother who was herself a Gaelic poet and singer, his background remained strongly Highland. When he writes

'Tis distance gives enchantment to the view
and robes the mountain in its azure hue

he is echoing the proverb *is gorm na cnuic a tha fada uainn* – blue are the hills of faraway. As he worked his way through university by tutoring children in vacations, he returned again and again to Argyll, finding at his father's old home of Kirnan

One rose of the wilderness left on its stalk,
To show where a garden had been.

Most of his work was done in the South – among other achievements he was instrumental in setting up the University of London; a contemporary graciously praised him as "the least Scotch of Scotchmen". As far as I can discover he never wrote in his native tongue. Maybe he'd have been glad to know that long afterwards Kirnan would become the home of a celebrated plant-collector, who wanted a 'blue lawn' and so produced *Gentiana MacAulayii*.

Three men, their lives widely separated in experiences and overlapping each other in time, their backgrounds so widely different, together form a mosaic of unity and variety – a century of poetry at the moment of the Industrial Revolution. Each of them carries us a step nearer the present, away from the green bracken hiding Druimliaghart, past the ruins of Ruthven, and Kirnan lost to its laird through the disasters of American trade and revolution. Of them all, it is Duncan of the Songs who has the most to say to us, if we knew how to listen. We are mostly ignorant of him, of his art, of his subjects. The sorry tale is summed up in the fate of that Ben Dorain 'pipe-well', as Duncan's 1912 editor tells it:

The well was, according to tradition, a spring rising out of the mountain to the height of a foot or two. So it was a delight to others beside the poet, till a Sassunach (Englishman) wandering in these parts, and moved by what spirit it is not easy to say, rammed his stick into the orifice and stopped the jet forever.

Perhaps it will some day break out again – perhaps it has even done so already unobserved; and perhaps there will be Gaelic poets to welcome it back. Springs are remarkably durable things.

21

Frontier Town

IN HIGH summer Inveraray is one more snarled knot of traffic on the road to the West, delightful though its eighteenth-century townscape looks from across the loch. The Great Inn entertained Johnson, Boswell, Burns, Keats – what would they make of today's multitudes swarming to tour the Castle? In wintertime it is more like the place they knew, though even then there are strange novelties.

The lights beckon, the dark hills shelter, one night's snow has silenced the street; some way each side of the town, odd wide ramps extend into the loch – not exactly jetties or fishing piers. The only speck of colour lies at the foot of a uniformed figure on the Green – a single blood-red wreath of poppies.

Impossible to explain to Mr Boswell that the Soldier is a war memorial, the ramps survive from Combined Operations training, stray concrete rectangles in Glen Shira remain from Polish Army encampments. If the town strikes today's visitors as an atom of cultured planning astray in a wilderness, such names as Eisenhower, Mountbatten and Montgomery among earlier droppers-in must cause bewilderment.

Inveraray grew with the Campbells, who arrived from Loch Awe around the fifteenth century. A shapeless thatched settlement huddled around a towerhouse near the river, focus of increasing political power, visited by James IV and Mary Queen of Scots. The Campbells may well have entered Argyll as followers of a thirteenth-century bishop from Carrick in Ayrshire, home of the Bruces, which might explain both their adherence to Robert I and their liking for the personal name Gillespie (*Gill'easbuig*, 'servant of the Bishop', oddly anglicised into 'Archibald'). If one takes their surname literally, *Cam beul* as 'crooked mouth', perhaps it implies an alien dialect; later opponents had no hesitation in equating it with 'paleface speak with forked tongue'.

A deal of nonsense has been written about Campbells as a vast homogeneous body. Other clans maintained stronger links and closer harmony. No Campbell chief was ever elected; the knights of Loch Awe upheld feudal procedures with an enthusiasm detested by those they dislodged. James IV opened an immense prospect by authorising his Chancellor, the second Earl, to resettle coastal lands forfeited by the Lord of the Isles. The settlement was incomplete when King and Earl died together at Flodden, although a network of kinsmen had spread over the western coasts.

The whole web twitched at any touch, but the sub-agents of the royal agent developed their own links for survival in hostile environments. When local interests required them to diverge from official policy, they sat quiet and minded their own business, and the earls showed due caution in resenting such thrawn resistance.

The outlying agents were not an army of occupation but a band of middle-management administrators, answerable to distant authority, dependent on local goodwill. When the eighth Earl became a Marquis, his clansmen were anything but united behind him. In December 1644 he fled by sea as Montrose's army swept down Glen Shira; two months later his galley's abrupt departure gave his forces their first inkling that Montrose was again upon them, swooping upon Inverlochy where Campbells fell 'like reaped corn'. The survivors never felt quite the same again about their leader. A fervent Protestant, he exacted Charles II's oath to uphold the Covenant before crowning him at Scone; "Ou-aye", said the clan, "and where's the King now? Away to the Low Countries, him and his brother, and our man at Inveraray squinting a welcome to the Englishes and their Cromwell."

Charles was no sooner restored in England than he had Argyll beheaded. The Marquis's son, an active royalist granted the earldom, was presently driven into exile where he plotted revolution with the Duke of Monmouth – a plot so transparent, so bungled in execution, that it cost both leaders their lives and farther split Clan Campbell.

England had Judge Jeffreys, Scotland had a near-hysterical Privy Council instructing their man on the spot, the Marquis of Atholl, to

> destroy what you can to all who joined any manner of way with Argyll. All...who are not come off on your or Breadalbane's

advertisement, are to be killed or disabled from ever fighting again; and burn all houses except honest men's, and destroy Inveraray and all the castles, and what you cannot undertake, leave to those that come after you ... Let the women and children be transported to remote islands...

Fortunately Atholl was almost as incompetent as Argyll, with less excuse. A ten-year-old at Kilberry, sentenced in his half-brother's absence, was saved by his foster-parents; some Campbell lairds were hanged, some exiled. Kilberry senior had earlier demonstrated the outliers' detachment from mainstream policy.

Weary of marching his tenants away to fight whoever was Argyll's latest target, a call to arms in 1647 found him reluctantly at Tarbert where he encountered his brother-in-law MacDonald of Largie, on a like errand for the other side. The commanders adjourned for a brotherly dram, another for the road, "How's my sister? Here's to her..."

Morning broke in blessed quiet. Two elderly gentlemen rubbed their aching brows and looked around for their troops, who had left without them.

It was acutely embarrassing, but Largie had the answer. He seized that dangerous opponent Kilberry and carried him prisoner to Kintyre. The Lady of Largie, née Campbell of Kilberry, was less than delighted, having begun her spring cleaning. As the contents of cellar and larder dwindled she made life a little uneasy. Thereupon her brother escaped, gallantly kidnapping Largie single-handed.

Mrs Campbell, née MacDonald, was even less pleased. She and her daughters had withstood a three-day siege by Islesmen, only broken when she lowered them a barrel of new ale with the message that she had plenty more malt and a good well under the tower. They drank up and left to find an easier prey – but to think of her brother and her husband carousing meanwhile – !

So they returned to Largie, and back soon after. It might have continued indefinitely had not MacNeill of Gigha intercepted the erratic boat and, being a tiresome idealist, threatened to denounce both pacifists to their respective commanders. Luckily he fell in love with one of Kilberry's girls and so joined the stay-at-home league.

So much for 'unalterable hostility between clans'. Few clans were the monoliths of later belief, battering each other like dinosaurs at a chief's command. Feuds there were aplenty, within clans as much as outside, blood-feuds, boundary squabbles; chiefs tried to maintain a concord. A clan might adopt a stance contrary to its chief's; in 1745 there were as many anti-Hanoverian (if not outright Jacobite) Campbells as inert MacDonalds. Threats of reprisal hounded both towards commitment.

So much has been said about 1715 and (especially) 1745 that we overlook long periods of unrest, 1709, 1719, 1726 – and before them the seventeenth-century upheavals, all underlain by profound unease at loss of control over the nation's affairs.

Bigotry, self-serving guile and treachery came of the Union of the Crowns; as Union of the Parliaments loomed, many saw it as the last hope to escape resentful southern neglect. Queen Anne's great minister, the second Duke, took part in arranging the 1707 Act of Union, but its results so disturbed him that within ten years he narrowly failed to have it annulled. Others favoured more direct action.

Archibald Campbell of Knockbuy, merchant of Glasgow, was clapped into Dunbarton Castle in 1715 at his anxious father's behest. Soon afterwards he retired to Lochfyneside and took up farming, betraying no hint of rebel thoughts until 1742 when a muddle creeps into his accounts: "I think I gott a Guinie from him the day Achanbreck and Lochiel came here". Campbell of Auchinbreck was an overt Jacobite, who with Lochiel was canvassing support for Prince Charles Edward. Knockbuy, however, held a militia commission in 1745 and commanded a company in Rannoch, with Colin of Glenure. Both Campbells found urgent business elsewhere, the night the Stewarts raided Blair Atholl; both were off-duty when Appin survivors got home from Culloden. Courtmartialled for absence, Knockbuy made a spirited defence; how could an aged man of 52 keep the Moor in wild April weather? He lived, unscathed, to 97; his friend was less fortunate. Colin had volunteered for administration after 1746; he 'did not like to be idle'. As Crown Factor for forfeited Appin lands, he was suspected of rebel sympathies and a warrant was issued. Before it could be served on him, he was dead, shot from ambush as he rode through the Lettermore woods to Ballachulish.

The killer was never found. Allan *Breac* Stewart, 'out' in '45, sometime of the French Army, trailed his coat nearby. He was indicted and outlawed, but disappeared. Nobody in Appin thought him guilty; another name is whispered still but never revealed.

Duncan Bàn MacIntyre, Glenure's foster-brother, composed a noble lament; kinsmen demanded revenge. The warrant was set aside – some tragic blunder.

Two days later Allan Breck's fosterer, James Stewart in Acharn, was arrested and charged with art and part in the crime. His cry on hearing of the death – "Lord bless us, was he shot?" – was held proof of guilty knowledge. He may have recalled an illicit meeting for target-practice at 'blackcocks', a common byename for Campbells in their dark tartan which alone was not banned. As a well-known leader of the local *Maquis*, James was every way in peril.

Legendary rancour surrounds his trial. Today he might have been convicted of conspiracy to defeat the ends of justice; he stood trial when nobody knew the Jacobite threat was over. George II and his Prime Minister visited Hanover until after the verdict; the death of a government agent could signal a new rising.

It was first proposed to try James in Edinburgh, but doubts arose; would any Lowland jury give justice to a Highland rebel? How could witnesses be brought to the city except as prisoners, how could their evidence be fairly presented through interpreters? Inveraray was the normal circuit-town for Highland cases. It should be taken there, before two judges and the Lord Justice-General who customarily sat at least one day in every circuit session. The Duke of Argyll had lost his heritable jurisdictions, like everyone else, in 1748, but he was a law graduate of Glasgow and Utrecht, a jurist of international acclaim – what signal would his absence send? He wrote to the Lord Chancellor:

> I cannot fear any partiality of the jury in favour of the persons accused, but I have some apprehension that in England some may observe the great number of persons in the jury of the same name as the gentleman who has been murdered...unavoidable, unless the Sheriff should affectedly pick out other names, which will be difficult to do.

He meant, of course, that of those qualified by landowning, most would be Campbells. Forty-three, twenty-two of them of the clan, were summoned, all Glenure's kinsmen were excluded, Stewart of Appin and MacLaine of Lochbuie were excused; of the fifteen jurors empanelled, eleven were named Campbell. The prosecutors eyed them uneasily.

Throughout the trial the uneasiness persisted. The Lord Advocate wrote that the state of the country made it imperative "to convince these barbarians that they must either subvert this government or submit to it". After three days, the jury retired for five long hours. In Sir James Fergusson's words,

> If, as is often alleged, James Stewart's condemnation had been decided in advance, it could certainly have been secured with less trouble, expense and fatigue, and the mere demonstration of justice could have been equally impressive and much less tedious.

This is the assessment of a modern historian and lawyer, a man descended from one of the judges and from Counsel on both sides.

The trial was held in the old church beside the tower, surrounded by building works. The new Court-house, the three-storey block near the Inn, was still unbuilt, its successor (now the successful Jail Museum) undreamed of. In earlier days a capital charge could not have been heard in a place of worship, but there was nowhere else large enough for the flock of lawyers. As for respectable lodgings, even his Grace lacked these in his half-built house.

A charge of art and part should not be heard before its principal, but no principal was to be found. For national security, for political expediency, possibly even for complicity, James was duly hanged at Ballachulish. A cairn marks the gallows-site, another in Lettermore covers Colin's deathspot.

The neat white town is all new since those days, its bygone life best traced in Neil Munro's loving descriptions. Canny merchants, ruffling gallants, girls in shawls and ladies in silk, step from his pages to steal through the streets. Candlelight glows on a snowy windowsill; a fiddle is tuned; a metal bar, let fall in a garage, rings like a sword. The town stirs gently in its sleep as the flakes drift down on the poppies.

In the night of 5-6 November 1975 Inveraray Castle burned, its upper floors almost totally destroyed, priceless treasures lost.

A Culloden pike enabled the Duke to puncture overburdened plaster ceilings; next day there were still three boiling feet of black water in the basement. The Clan's whole heritage was threatened. It was fitting, therefore, that the worldwide Clan rallied to restore the building, repair the contents, clean the surviving pictures, even extend the displays to give due space to Combined Ops HQ. Evidently the much criticised 'clan spirit' is not lost.

22

The Harried Nest

THE NORTH-EASTER is enough to make your lungs ache, hashing down the Sound of Jura from northern snows. The sea, an angry blue, is striped with crests that drive stiffly into the black skerries. Here on the ridge above the empty houses one is tempted back to the shelter of the fields, but even there the dry rushes flail; beyond them, Small Isles Bay is a scurry of foam. Westward the brown land rises, ridge behind rolling ridge, until the three quartz-cones of the Paps rise sheer into the sky. Evan MacColl, gazing on them from Iona, wrote

> Jura's sister-summits three
> Love in the path of stars to be

and on this March day they could easily reach a star or two.

Beyond Ardfarnal lies the horseshoe sweep of Lowlandman's Bay, curling past the former school to the old lighthouse station. At its far end a cluster of red roofs sits aslant a green shoulder; one chimney smokes.

If we were on the lee side of Jura, or sailing past its western shore, there would be no house-smoke, no cattle – only deer and wild goats and the giant combmarks of furrows cloaked in bracken. Nobody lives there, only slender pony-trails cross the central ridge. The people left within living memory – too few men to handle a boat, too few women to help in childbirth. Nobody evicted them, they vanished under pressures too complex to be overcome.

Said Cook to my mother, defending the mysterious shrinkage of a dinner-service,

"Hech, mem, now and again one dwindles!"

Flora was speaking a parable, the fate of a thousand townships. From the

Ardmenish fields comes a roar of wings and a wild crying; tossing into the wind go the greylag geese, stretching their necks against the gale, wheeling to stranger-free pastures.

One family worked Ardmenish in the 1970s, when I saw it last; long walls and fallen gables told of happier times. The empty shells brought inescapably to mind those loaded words 'crofters' and 'clearances'. Evan MacColl again, this time in his native tongue:

Tha Gaidheil 'g am fògradh
Mar cheò bharr do shleibhtean,
'S ma lean riut cinn-fheadhn',
'S ann air caoirich is fèidh!

'The Gael is driven off like the mist from your mountains; you're left with the lairds and their sheep and deer.'

Things are seldom all that simple. Most 'crofters' are later than most 'clearances' (I hear the snorts of disbelief; I must go roundabout to explain).

Irish laws recognised two kinds of land-tenure. There were free farmers, holding land in return for armed service to a king, much like feudal knights, with the important difference that their tenure was for seven years, the king supplying the initial seedcorn and cattle as in English 'steelbow' or french *métayage*.

The tenant returned a third of the increase annually, in kind, restoring the equivalent of the 'capital' at the full term. Such a tenure may underlie the Scots system of tacks, leases for a term of years whereby one man held several farms, providing horses, seeds and ploughshares to working tenants. They paid him rent in labour and produce, and he in turn remitted cash to his superior. In vast holdings such as ducal estates, tacksmen were essential; perishable foodstuffs could not be got from Tiree to Inveraray.

The other ancient tenure was the group-farm. Here a kinship held the land, effectively in perpetuity (since the whole group must perish before possession lapsed). Though primitive and resistant to change, the system operated throughout the eighteenth century. While it seems incredible that it could endure from Dalriadic times, it is equally unlikely to have begun in the Age of Improvement. The eighth Duke of Argyll explained it to Queen

Victoria as they drove past Auchnagoul and Auchindrain; in her *Highland Journal* she is both shocked and impressed to find it so like practices in her Indian Empire.

The community of around a dozen families, possibly deriving from the *dearbh-fine*, ruled itself under an elected spokesman. With the total rent fixed by the landowner, the group decided how many partners to have, and whether to admit new members. Three arable fields, worked in rotation, were divided into strips for which the partners drew lots annually, some good and some poorer ground in each lot. Grazings were held in common, the 'Soum' (total carrying-capacity) precisely known in terms of cattle and adjusted for other stock (one horse = 1.5 cows, 3 sheep = 2 cows). There were communal peatbanks, and shielings where the young people camped, herding the cattle away from the corn, making butter and cheeses.

The township might contain cottars, sub-tenants working part-time for the partners and often practising some useful skill such as weaving or shoemaking; a widow might be supported by the whole group, getting her main meal with each household by turn and acting as midwife-babysitter. The houses were set on the poorest ground, built of stones cleared from the fields and erected by communal labour; the landowner might be required to provide roof-timbers. The last mainland community of this style is now the farming museum of Auchindrain near Inveraray.

It was a tough but cheerful life, with pipers, fiddlers and singers, dancing on summer nights, impromptu *ceilidhe* (sessions of storytelling and song) in winter, when the rule was, "First tale from the host, tales from the guest until morning", (the householder was expected to set the tone for proceedings). It was a reasonable living, but some necessities no township could grow – salt, iron, tar. With little surplus production to barter and part of the rent due in cash, curious expedients appear in eighteenth-century rentals – 'a barrel of butatas', even *tobacka* or *silk hancrorchifs* from a member of a shoreside holding (wine arrived in quiet bays annually: "Send more bottels, there is no bottels left here.")

Coin was always scarce; it appeared mainly with the cattle drovers who traversed the countryside with almost the status of heralds, buying livestock from the townships and returning long afterwards with the market proceeds. Men and women also trekked to the Lowlands for harvestwork or fishing, bringing a little money home – sometimes a 'Moydore' or a 'Guinie' to be credited through the accounts for years. Mutton, cheese and poultry were the commonest payments, but the communities moved effortlessly to a credit system when a group of lairds undertook large-scale cattle dealing, hiring a drover to work through Islay, Jura and Knapdale buying bullocks which were then grazed on inland farms until the midsummer Kilmichael Tryst. Thence they moved, in level drafts, to Crieff or Falkirk and on to England. The initial purchases were made with Bills of Exchange postdated to the autumn rent-day, by which time the cattle had been sold for a handsome profit. Unhappily the scheme was checked by an outbreak of rinderpest in England, just before 1745 and the rocketing rise in livestock prices which continued until Waterloo.

Rents also rose. New owners exploited forfeited estates and adopted a more luxurious lifestyle; some tenants supported exiled landlords while still trying to appease the new Factor (apt to demand cash, not butter or eggs). The population also rose, partly thanks to the enthusiastic welcome for smallpox-vaccination, while (despite the general adoption of potato-growing) foodstocks barely increased at all.

In 1769 Tiree had 1550 inhabitants, in 1787 there were 2034, mostly women and children (of 57 men enlisted in 1750, only twelve returned). Recalling empty lands seen during service in America, the ex-soldiers led their families away from the Duke's neat new fishing-villages and his theories of kelp-burning and fisheries to enhance living standards. Most landlords believed 'a numerous tenantry' equalled wealth. Few farmed for themselves, relying on staggered payment of kain-rents – butter, cheese, mutton – for their household needs. They offered inducements to check emigration, such as slight reductions in rent or improvement grants; they started spinning-schools, lintmills, lacemaking, to absorb excess female labour. Gangs of women dug every yard of workable ground, mainly for potatoes, working with spades where no plough could go; their green ridges ride high up the hillsides yet.

The tacksmen bore the brunt of the squeeze; it was they who saw the rising hunger, the soldier's widow, the disabled seaman; they wrote to kinsmen overseas, chartered ships and led whole glens to cross the seas. New occupants had to be enticed into empty grounds, encountering here and there an old woman who had refused to go and who felt the full weight of the saying, *Is e 'n dealachadh-beò a ni'n leòn goirt* – it's parting from the living that's the sore wound.

At least improvements might now be extended. Lowland farmers were enticed to demonstrate their superior skills; Knockbuy let one of his hill cattlefarms to a 'Low Country sheep herd', partly to assess the result, partly because in his nineties he could barely see to keep his accounts. The 'sheep herd' soon departed, and an ex-drover restocked the grazings.

Distant governments offered grants for fishing, crafts, and kelp-burning (to produce potash while the wars cut out Spanish barilla). An uproar over emigrant-ship conditions did more to check emigration, by raising fares and limiting overcrowding.

The old system had discouraged change, so new tenancies were granted to individuals, each with a separate house on grounds defined by long parallel dykes. These are the roadside crofting townships we see today. Within them, traditions of shared working struggled to survive.

Wool was something the hills could produce, from big Blackface sheep rather than the little petted runts women had kept as pets. The big sheep needed one wholetime shepherd and replaced a gaggle of disaffected peasantry. Patrick Sellars' Morvern demonstration of his Sutherland successes was less savage than Strathnaver – fewer soldiers, less houseburning – but just as effective.

Some communities somehow escaped the worst. When Kilian was cleared to make an Improver's farm, nearby Auchindrain opened its doors to the evicted families. Over the hill at Kenmore, one of the Duke's fishing villages throve.

Its houses were placed trimly around a net-drying green, staring impolitely into each others' doors, but pleasantly set among good farmland. Among the early tenants was Dugald MacColl, an Appin man come south to make estate roads (he later became a general road contractor). He was a famous traditional singer, his wife was a storyteller and poetess. Dugald taught his children to appreciate nature, taking them to good viewpoints, showing them birds and animals. He owned books – Burns's poems, Blind Harry's epic *The Wallace* – and once bought a book pedlar's entire pack, sight unseen.

His seventh son and youngest child was christened Evan and called Eòghann at home. He was a naturalist from babyhood, reportedly defending birds' nests 'like a little knight errant'; he catches the very rhythm of a skylark's song:

Till, m'eun ceutach,
Till, mu'n téid thu
Far nach feud mi
Tuille d'éisdeachd,
'S mu' m fàg treubhan
Binn nan speura
Air bheag gleusaidh
'N cruitean fein a dh' fhòglum bhuait!

Come, my bonny bird,
Come, lest you go
Where I'd never
Hear you more;
Though the sweet host
Of heaven failed,
With a little tuning
The very harps could learn from you!

Evan got his first schooling from a flogging brute of a Dominie, provided by the Duke at £10 a year and lodged with each pupil's family in turn. He taught exclusively in English, punishing every whispered word in the children's only language with blows and a horse's skull hung around the offender's neck until it was needed for another sinner. Luckily for the young MacColls, their father brought a young mission teacher to stay for a year before going to Jamaica, and from him the children learned to read and write Gaelic.

Evan produced his first song secretly, teaching it to another boy and hiding outside the Widow's House in Kenmore to judge its reception. When the whole *ceilidh* applauded he "felt myself a Bard, and was supremely happy".

He grew up working the land, roadmaking, handling a fishing skiff. When peace came in 1815 and the cattle trade collapsed, banks broke, businesses collapsed, Evan's family joined the new flow of emigration. At the last minute he stayed behind, resolving to remain until he could "give my countrymen something to remember me by", and making contact with other self-taught writers such as Hugh Miller, other authors from the brothers Sobieski Stuart to Dr Robert Chalmers.

In 1836 his promised book appeared, with his own 'lament for the living':

> *Air son gach còmhnuidh 'sam faighte 'n aoigheachd,*
> *Tha'n larach dhuaichnidh – o! uaigh na fèileachd!*
> *Mar nead na smeoraich am bun na geuige,*
> *An déidh do'n fheòc'lan a h-àl a reubadh!*

> Instead of every welcoming house
> Disfigured ruins – o graves of bounty!
> Like the thrush's nest at the sapling foot
> After the polecat has stolen the brood.

The MP for Argyll presently found Evan a post in the Liverpool Customhouse – a strange world but one where he found happiness with a Cumberland wife; he also gained insights into the next disaster for the Celtic lands, the 1840s Potato Blight. Again packed ships left Liverpool, again news came of new Argyll evictions.

Evan went too, to visit his family in Canada, returning only to pack and follow. He came back later on holiday, walking through Scotland: "Forres, Nov 15 1888. Dine with the MacLeans of North Cottage – a fine family from my own country. Gaelic – music – very happy."

Today a cairn stands on Kenmore Point to the memory of the Lochfyneside Bard, and a thrush in the woods above sings *Eòghann, Eòghann, beannachd leat, beannachd leat!* Fare-ye-well, Evan, and farewell all you singers of the glens where the hearths are cold.

On that word of *cold*, where the Ardmenish track dips to a ford, there is a sudden plunge into invisible kneedeep ice. I knew, but I'd forgotten.

Here a drover was found dead, robbed of money anxiously awaited to pay last year's arrears of rent; a frightful and unforgotten crime.

The wild geese cry, the snell wind blows, Jura's sister-summits glisten with ancient tears. In the scrub oaks above the ford a warbler utters one tentative trill. The summer birds are back as the winter birds shape to fly. Some day, who knows, even the men may return.

Mi 'Fagail na Tire
('My Leaving of the Land')

The way I went some spite had planned,
to know the homes of other men,
the time I turned to leave the land,
it was not well with me then.

That these old headlands falling back
could draw such dim eyes to their hold,
that hills beyond a steamer's track
could hurt so sore, I was not told.

There Sleea swung away from me,
hidden by hills I never crossed.
I had not heard that rock and scree
and rain-scarred slope were precious lost.

My eyes on Laggan, and the sound
of homely waters far astern;
that day the ancient grief I learned
of songs sung lightly, in my turn.

George Campbell Hay, from Wind on Loch Fyne, *Oliver & Boyd, 1948*

Note

'Sleea' is Sliabh Gaoil

23

The Soldier's Road

SHE IS on equal terms with Ben More of Mull, peak to peak across the sea. She beckons to Benderloch, the royal footprint on Dunadd points her out; a remote unattainable queen, she draws the eye northward from Tarbert. West in Knapdale we see her step out from behind lesser hills with her snow-coif gleaming. *Cruachan Beann, mo Chruachan Beann* – watchword and rallying cry, the steep, bright, triple-crested mountain.

The road northwards from Inveraray climbs out on a bare hill-shoulder, and there's Loch Awe. The sudden gleam of wide waters checks the traveller, but it is the soaring dark slope beyond that holds him. There stands Cruachan, all of her, the thin scar of a hydro-electric dam merely adding scale and height. The hollow mountain, hiding a vast power-station, remains the mistress of magic.

Her name was a war-cry; *"Cruachan!"* as the dark plaids were thrown aside for battle; that triple maidenhead was the cynosure, the core of the homeland. "It's a far cry to Loch Awe," we said, meaning that we were out on a limb somewhere and must stand fast, and the opposition of the time returned the word with interest to mean that the Campbell mafia was for once at a disadvantage.

In the gulch of Brander on her western flank the MacDougalls nearly did for Robert Bruce; on her east side stood the MacGregor keep of Glen Strae; the northernmost corrie provided the MacIntyres' crown rent of a snowball in June. Under the sweeping skirts of her, where land and water meet, rise the dark walls of Kilchurn that Black Colin of Glenorchy built. A necklace of green islands lies across the loch, from Fraoch Eilean whose castle was entrusted to the MacNaughtons by Alexander III, to Innishail with its carved stones around a sanctuary-church.

The loch, Y-shaped at its northern end, bends south-westerly to cleave the low brown hills. Cairns great and small overlook it, tracks lead to old crossings guarded by forts on knobby ridges. All down the shores there are cairnlike islets, stone-dumps built up as platforms for wolf-proof and human-proof huts, crannogs made and remade from the earliest times until no time ago. Far down the east shore on a bigger rock stands Innis Chonnaill, the oldest known Campbell castle with strong hints of a twelfth-century origin. Across the water the Avich river drains its own castled loch whence a track threads through the String of Lorn past the cairn where Cailean Mór, the first Campbell knight, fell in battle.

South again is Kilmaha, a chapel site and an early rock-cut icon (possibly representing the Desert Father, St Antony, but carved into such difficult rock that I only found it at a second visit). Across at the far south-eastern corner, Finchairn Castle throws its shadow over the water buttercups and uphill in the farmyard lies the huge *Fianna-charn*, the Fingalians' Mound. From there the old road, now drowned in trees, ran directly to Kilneuair – the Church of the Yews, 'Sanct Colmys Kirke in Glasrie' which might just be the lost *Cella Diuni* that Adomnan mentions in passing. It was the head church of the wide Glassary parish, with a noted market at its gates, until Kilmichael replaced it. The old track still runs past and climbs the hills towards Auchindrain.

The loch ends in a lagoon, the Lodan, where a steamer-pier sags into green water and dark woods fall steeply to meet their reflections. Up through those woods I clambered once, catching at tree-trunks, to see where eighty years before that, two boys out rabbiting had found a cache of bronze spearheads. My guide was wondering if he would recognise the place he'd been shown, forty years back, by the younger brother of one of the hunters, before the Forestry Commission began planting. He halted by a great perched boulder, hesitated, turned away – and I heard him say in a puzzled voice, "What's a bit of cart harness doing up here?"

He held on his palm a thickly patinated green circle – no harness but a bronze bracelet. This cannot happen, one does not stroll back after eighty years and collect more bits of a prehistoric hoard. We knelt and brushed away pine-needles, and there below the rock lay a second armlet, a knife, some lumps of copper ore and three small axeheads. You can see them together with the surviving spear (another was lost) and a hollow gouge, in the National Museums of Scotland in Edinburgh. I long to know who hid them and why, how he got there, where he went, trading new axes for old;

did he turn up regularly, so that you set aside your worn tools for him, as we used to set aside cooking pots until the working tinkers re-appeared with the spring?

Loch Awe has been a thoroughfare since the first man found it, opening a way through bleak hills or dense forest. War galleys drove in the wake of war canoes, and after them lumbered the flat-bottomed boats that gave many a horseman a welcome short cut between Crinan and the Tay.

Above the Lodan stands a fortified crag called the Chief's Fort, *Dùn Tòiseich* – so small, he cannot have been lord of more than the nearby fields, but he did command an old green road that winds from Torran to Inverliever. The Torran end is marked by a big standing stone on which some missionary has cut crosses – tactfully sanctifying a relic his converts cherished. Along the track lies the Angel's Well, its story lost, and beyond that again is the rock-cut cistern called *Tobar na Bile*.

There are house ruins beside the Well of the Holy Trees, and a cupmarked boulder; one building lies plumb east-and-west and might have been a chapel in its time. Certainly there was a graveyard, in which was found a plaque of ivory – boxlid or book cover – which was believed to have dropped from Heaven. It was long known as 'Barbreck's Bone'; it too is now in Edinburgh, but formerly it worked wonders, healing man and beast. The Well itself had power; the women of Inverliever watched it for news of their menfolk's welfare in war, for it ebbed and flowed with their fortunes.

Many a time the Well repaid watching; every little glen sent out its raiding parties, to follow a chief or settle private feuds with the lifting of a few cattle. Not all the warboats of MacNaughton or Campbell could check the to-and-fro of those who knew every pass or steered with muffled oars in the dark of the moon.

In 1725 a law forbade the Highlanders to own any offensive weapon. At the same time military engineers arrived to construct roads through the hills. As a good gun or a grandfather's sword had almost mystical importance, and as the roads were obviously meant to speed troop movements in future insurrections, most natives regarded both developments with equal loathing. They found the roads useful for importing old guns from European battlefields, battered rusty things nobody regretted surrendering, and the construction camps were worth the occasional quick raid – for stores, to educate the young entry, or for the hell of it – but there was little other pleasure to be got out of the new activities. By degrees some army units established good relations with the civil population (in the curious way of Scottish and English armies anywhere) and small companies of local men were even enrolled as police, under their own officers, to check thefts of cattle.

Gradually these 'independent companies' evolved into a kind of militia; they were equipped with a new tartan, based on the Campbell plaid (black, green and blue) from which they were nicknamed *Am Freiceadan Dubh*, the 'Black Watch', to distinguish them from red-coated Regulars. In 1739 they were taken on to the Army List as the 43rd Regiment of the Line, soon renumbered as the 42nd, to become the oldest surviving Highland regiment.

The first units were bands of kinsmen, almost an echo of the ancient *Féinn*. Their conduct was governed by brotherhood and family pride, not by the harsh discipline of the day, and something of this proud tradition remains to the present. Their quality was soon apparent and other Highland units were formed. After 1746 and a Disarming Act with new and stricter clauses – not only weapons, but the wearing of the kilt and the music of the pipes were banned – army service became the only outlet for warlike instincts and the only lawful means to wear traditional dress and hear the sounds that were the very voice of the hills. By 1766 Pitt himself recognised the transformation of 'pestiferous clans' into a national asset:

> I sought for merit wherever it was to be found; it is my boast that I was the first minister who looked for it and found it in the mountains of the north. They served with fidelity as they fought with valour, and conquered for you in every part of the world.

He was of course addressing the House of Commons. A Scot working in London, who chanced to be in the Park when the 42nd was parading before George III, was drawn to the sound and went back to his lodgings in tears, crying "I have a country, after all!" Some generals were cynical – even Wolfe, who had tested Highland mettle at Culloden, and who was to die in the arms of a plaided soldier, remarked that 'it was no great harm if some of them fell'; despite such doubts, the regiments marked a new era. For generations individual highlanders had gone to serve in European armies (MacKay's Regiment, from Sutherland and Caithness, was a core unit in William of Orange's campaigns); now their worth was accepted at home. A little money trickled back to their families, news came of territories open to settlement. As they moved from Canada to India, from the West Indies to China, the soldiers extended their knowledge of the world. Already many Argyll men had gone to Jamaica, first brought to their attention in the aftermath of the Darien tragedy; now, as the population overflowed at home, many veterans came back only to lead their families to the emigrant ships.

We have long been accustomed to sending our young men to war; call them mercenaries, if you like – say they fought in other men's causes, condemn all militaristic ideas – but do not imagine that it cost us nothing to see them go, and do not slight, in our hearing, the memory of our dead.

Sometimes, in a green dusk, Loch Awe gleaming like steel under the sunset wind, there goes along the Inverliever road the sound of a trotting horse. A little old grey-headed man rides by, a sword on his hip and a feather bonnet on his head, and he growls as he goes, "Ninety-third, Ninety-third, damn all that eagerness!"

Field Marshal Lord Clyde was not born a Campbell. His father was a Glasgow cabinet-maker by the name of Macliever and his mother was a Campbell from Islay. Local tradition makes Inverliever his home, and claims that some misfortune connected with 1745 had sent him away to the city. A Campbell uncle offered to get Colin – and perhaps his younger brother, although this is unclear – into the army, and presented him, or them, to the 'grand old' Duke of York, the Commander-in-Chief. The Royal Duke had Colin's commission made out in the uncle's name, to the boy's fury; but many another had borrowed a name and a tartan in the past, so he swallowed his pride and took up his posting.

From Vimiera to Walcheren, to Corunna, Barossa and Vittoria he marched, then to China and long-forgotten campaigns in India, eventually to the governorship of Peshawar. At last he found himself in the Crimea to take command of a newly formed Highland Brigade, made up of the 42nd, 79th (Cameron Highlanders) and 93rd (Sutherland, soon to become Argyll and Sutherland Highlanders). As they forded the Alma behind him, another half-Campbell general flanked them – Scarlett of Scarlett's Horse, whose mother's home was at Lochgilphead. They halted on the ridge beyond the river and the new Brigadier addressed his men – not in the flowery terms of 'Ossian':

> "Now, men, you are going into action. Remember this, whoever is wounded – I don't care what his rank is – must lie where he falls until the bandsmen come to attend to him. No soldier must go carrying off wounded men; if any man does such a thing his name will be stuck up in his parish church. Don't be in a hurry about firing. Be steady. Keep silence. Aim low. Now, men, the army will watch us. Make me proud of my Highland Brigade!"

Two days later he ordered a parade. He had asked Lord Raglan, 'as a great favour', to let him wear a feather bonnet like his men, and had one secretly made with a hackle combining all three regiments' colours. The parade was nominally

> because the General was desirous of thanking them for their conduct on 20th (at the Alma). The square was formed and he rode into it with the bonnet on. No order or signal was given, but he was greeted with such a succession of cheers, again and again, that both the French and English armies were startled into a perfect state of wonder as to what had taken place.

Then came Balaklava, and an immortal phrase. The 'Thin Red Line' (but Russell, the war correspondent, had written "the thin red streak tipped with steel") was thin indeed, 550 men of the 93rd in two stretched ranks, with a hundred 'invalids' on their flank. Sir Colin went down the line:

> "Now, men, remember there is no retreat from here. You must die where you stand."

From the ranks, the voice of John Scott, right marker of No 6 Company:

"Ay, ay, Sir Co-lin, an' need be, we'll do that."

So they stood, against Russian cavalry ("Damn all that eagerness!") and fired their two volleys, and cheered. From that day the 93rd adopted the Glasgow cabinet-maker's son as one of themselves. Three years later, having gone straight from the Black Sea to India, they met him again on the Grand Trunk Road, marching towards Lucknow. Russell was there, covering the 'Great Mutiny' for the *Times*, and wrote, "They look on him as if he belonged to them, like their bagpipes – a property useful in war". He had struck a phrase that was no bad summary of a clan's view of a chief.

The pipes were soon to sound rescue-at-hand to the beleaguered Lucknow garrison, a sick woman crying out "Dinna ye hear them?"

As the force moved on to Cawnpore the General noted that "on this occasion was the sight beheld of 24-pounder guns advancing with the first line of skirmishers…"

These were the guns of the Naval Brigade, hauled by seamen and Highlanders together – a foretaste of the 'Plymouth Argylls' who would make a last stand at Singapore in this century. Within Cawnpore, when messenger after messenger had died attempting to summon help, the survivors were on the edge of despair. "In a moment, all was changed"; horses galloped over the bridge of boats as night fell; "as they came close under the ramparts it was seen that an old man with grey hair was riding at their head. 'It is Sir Colin!' The news spread like wildfire."

At another bridge that the 53rd, the Shropshires, had held all day, the 93rd were sent to relieve them. The Shropshires were not prepared to give ground to anyone, and the two regiments confronted each other. The old man rode up in a fury at this breach of discipline, but a brave soul in the 53rd drowned his opening remarks with a yell of "Three cheers for the General, boys!"

Again the irate General commenced his scolding, and again his voice was drowned…once more he essayed to rebuke…at length, finding it impossible, the stern countenance assumed for the occasion relaxed, and the veteran Chief turned away with a laugh. Sir Colin, it may be added, had just a few minutes before been

struck in the stomach by a spent ball, which had strength enough
to cut his wind for the moment...

The two regiments stood their ground and cheered the rest of the troops
across – Lancers, Sikhs and staff.

    Maybe the rider on the green road sometimes halts to rub his midriff
and allow himself a ghostly chuckle at the memory of those cheers.

24

To Knowing How

IN THE green hollow of Slockavullin, down-valley from Kilmartin, overlooking the ancient cairns, stands a blacksmith's forge. To it one day the farm horses hauled the laird's new Horseless Carriage. It squatted monstrous by the door while the smith wrought upon its innards by trial and error. At last it burst into life, and he watched it belch away towards the coach-house before going indoors to write a bill.

> To repairing the Motor Car...£5.5.0d.

That brought Himself along in a hurry. What the devil was this? Five guineas for a morning's work? He demanded details – and got them. The new account read:

To materials for repairing Motor Car	0.5.0d
To knowing how	5.0.0d
	£5.5.0d

And you can't say fairer than that.

Smiths have always Known How. In the legends they are wizards, controlling secrets of fire and cold iron, spellbinders – do they not turn stone into swords? – often the only healers of the wounds dealt by their weapons. They have replaced the older Men of Skills, the bronzesmiths called simply *cèard*, craftsman. All Scots named Caird – great shipbuilders, famous doctors – descend from some bygone *cèard*.

Today we use the name for the nomadic tinkers, no longer tinsmiths but often scrap dealers. They trek all summer, camping on such ancestral sites as remain to them (many have been barred, through prejudice or ignorance; others they avoid because the 'Settled People' have used and befouled them), finding seasonal work or gathering shellfish for market.

Some are remnants of broken clans, some perhaps descend from the oldest race, the hunters of the Middle Stone Age. They speak a Gaelic of their own, with strange words maybe older. When I meet them I remember the words Tacitus put into the mouth of Calgach the Spearman:

We, the last men on earth, the last of the free...

Far in the mists the first travelling men passed, carrying flint or axe-stones. Others brought Baltic amber or black jet and cannel-coal from Whitby or the Kintyre-Knapdale shores, to be made into amulets or broad bead-collars. These were more precious than gold to the Bronze Age 'Settled People' (who got gold in some copper-mines), for if you rub jet or amber between your hands you generate static electricity, enough to collect bronze-filings from a workbench or lift them from a wound.

MacAlpine's *Gaelic Dictionary* (1847) revealed that secret; under *sùigh*, 'to absorb, drink up' it quotes *shùigh an t-ombar an duradan a'm shùil* – 'the amber lifted the mote from my eye'. Somebody knew how, long ago.

There is a continuity in skills. Nineteenth-century tombstone makers worked the same quarries, and cut their flowing scripts into the same bluestone, as furnished medieval cross makers with the level-bedded schist that "carves like butter while the quarry-sap's in it" (as a modern mason told me). Among their flourishes and masonic symbols they have cut leafscrolls harking back to the High Crosses, as they in turn harked back to Norse plaitwork and Irish manuscripts, and through these to the hairspring tendrils and formalised masks of pre-Christian Celtic Europe.

If you look closely at eighth-century Gospels or prehistoric bronze mirrors, you may detect behind the strong freehand curves the compass markings of a strict geometrical layout; craft behind art, freedom born of skill. The tradition still lives, however dead a hand may fall upon it at times – Reformation that dismisses old art as Popery, modern copying that imitates where it cannot create.

Not every craftsman is an original artist, though technical ability can approach inspiration; watch a dykebuilder handle his raw material, hefting each stone and turning it, seeking its true bed and balance. A man with his craft literally in his fingertips can achieve flashes of genius, like the Tarbert boatbuilders who gave their parish church a timber roof noble as a clipper's hull within.

A country community needs many skills – dyeing, spinning, weaving; woodworking, tanning, shoemaking. Even today little businesses spring up in unexpected corners, anything from handbuilt carburettors to computer cottages. There is no lack of skills, nor is the custom of communal work wholly lost while all the shepherds meet to shear each farm's sheep by turn.

But it's quieter now; you hear less singing. Time was when every job had its song and its singer to set the pace and lighten the work. The women fulling webs had their leader to improvise scandalous verses as they damped and thumped, and to sing a praise-blessing over the finished plaid. The fishers pulled home with one voice raising an air and boat after boat taking up the chorus – coming down Small Isles Bay at nightfall towards the lamplit windows, a glint of silver from the bilge where the saithe lay – *Fhir a'Bhàta*, I hear you yet. This was the singing of the Gael as no concert platform hears it, the song growing out of the work and the work giving life to the song.

The shoreside crofts were never intended to supply all a family's needs or require all its working time. They are smallholdings, enough to supply some food and leave time for some earning. It is part of today's problem that casual earnings are scarce, either from seasonal work or from what I suppose one must call 'cottage industry', much as I dislike the taint of condescension in that phrase. Huge industry, brought in the wake of oil or whatever, is no answer either, unless the crofts are all replaced by concrete or quarry dust.

I remember a contractor complaining bitterly that he'd given work to every unemployed man in a district, and then: "One morning they simply didn't turn up – left me flat; when I got hold of a couple that night they gave me some idiotic spiel about seeing birds in the loch, so they'd gone to fish. What can you do with people like that?"

What indeed, if you cannot understand that your 'unemployed' were fishermen waiting for the diving gannets to signal the coming of herring shoals?

I'm sorry for those who devise new industries for us; theirs is a thankless task unless they know the land and its people. Nowadays the fishing boats have found new targets, and their crews stand less often against the seawall watching for foam spouts. They sail for more than herrings – for prawns, scallops, whitefish when quotas permit – and the catch goes direct to Paris or Madrid. The fleet has every gadget from radar to echo sounders, but still carries men who can find a way through fog by the colour of the sea, or listen to shoals of fish through a wire lowered into the depths. Tarbert boats make a brave showing when they leave – a wink of emerald as one draws astern, a ruby glow as she heads out to sea. *King Fisher*, *Morning Winds*, *Maireared*, their engines rumble over the quiet harbour; but the oldest people remember brown sails thronging the Narrows, as they remember the heart-throb of paddles when *Columba* or *Grenadier* churned up to the East Pier.

Those paddle steamers brought exiles home, and visitors, but it was the brown skiffs that landed the herring, the Silver Darlings. I can recall winter days when the gutting-tables ranged around the whole arc of the breastwall, and the girls' striped aprons were rigid with herring scales and blood, when knives flickered too fast to follow, little stout barrels oozed brine as they swung from the jib of a black-lum screw's crane, and thin spears of song rose to defy spears of sleet.

"Aweel," said an old man to me, "Efter the first 'oor the hands wiz dumb."

Above the new Fish Market sits the Castle. Its broken tower is all that remains of James IV's 'new work'; a broad girdling wall runs to a grassgrown keep. What lies below the grass is not yet revealed, but that keep was old when Robert I undertook improvements.

Robert Bruce knew Tarbert; here his fleet had crossed the land, here he held a parliament when much of Scotland was in enemy hands. In his last years, stricken by an illness some called leprosy (but other contemporaries, and he himself, attributed it to his "much hard lying" in the troublous years), he came down to inspect the works and make Tarbert a Royal Burgh. *Et pro factura unius cokete ad burgum de Tarbard* – to making a customs seal, token of leave to import and export – is noted in the oldest complete Exchequer Roll to survive, alongside details of the building works and the tradesmen's names.

Adam and Robert, masons (Robert built his section of wall too wide, upsetting the estimates); Neil and Patrick, smiths; John the carpenter, another Neil, plumber. Hugh Dulp made a mill; Gilbert 'MacKathil' (in fact

MacKay, he who had guided the King through Kintyre hills in 1307) supplied meal and cheese for the workforce; Copin Ulf, merchant, provided cloth and sacks. Brenn and his dogs guarded the timber-yard.

In August 1327 the old King arrived; there had been a fine to-do to have everything ready, new birch branches woven into the framework of a half-finished hall, sweet herbs to strew its floor. John del More, Clerk of the Kitchen, was frantically planning his menus and obtaining store beasts from the King's herdsman and the Queen's shepherd. And Robert was bringing guests as well – the bishop of St Andrews to consecrate a chapel, Sir James Douglas to keep the King company (maybe with talk of desperate times when young James had guddled trout to feed a royal family on the run). The good Sir James would soon carry his King's heart into battle against Spanish Saracens, throwing the casket ahead with his unforgotten "Lead on, brave heart, where thou wast ever used to be!" (Now they deny it, but it's difficult to forget.)

It was fine weather for that last holiday voyage from Cardross 'doon the watter'. Tarbert smiles in summer, when yachts crowd the bay and visitors throng the quayside. But every fishing port knows hard times – there was a Tarbert man who saw to the heart of it, John MacDougall Hay (father of George, whose verses adorn this book), author of an epic novel entitled *Gillespie*. It tells the bitter tale of a man caught between two cultures, a powerful, crowded story of greed and tragedy on which there falls at last "some dew of pity".

> In the sea-town which harbours a fishing fleet these are the footsteps
> of the men in the night which the women know – the trudge which
> tells of bleak shores and empty boats, the joyous ring of the steel-
> shod heels with which the younger men dint the pavement, crying
> aloud of herring, and another step – ominous, slow, shuffling, as
> men creep silently home. Women strain their ears, for the step may
> not stop at their door; and if it does not – why, there shall no longer
> be the big sea-boots to clean. On that step at the threshold hangs life
> and death; ill it go by or enter in? The families who have given tithe
> of their folk to the sea have heard it pass away up the lane into a
> silence which, louder than trumpetings, they shall never forget.

What a moment is that when the step comes to the door and it is opened and 'Oh, is it you?' cries the wife or daughter, and, overcome with joy, drags in the wearied man! In another house the wife is lying staring into the dark waiting, waiting for the feet that will never come.

Like Gaelic poets of old, the Hays, father and son, drew their imagery from the landscape that nourished them. Here, again from *Gillespie*, is a rare savage winter:

The terns left early, and gulls were scavenging inland. Autumn waded through a roaring equinox that blistered the fleet. The land was filled with the boom of rain-lashed gales. Old Sandy prophesied dire weather. 'I saw three suns in the sky, an' the win's shifted oot o' too mony airts'. The brown nets on the poles along the Harbour were rotting, and could not be dried. The last birds to leave were the herons, which had watched on the shore in immobile gauntness as if carved out of grey rock. They flapped their heavy way like winged stone, leaving the loch empty.

A savage nihilism of storms beat upon the town. They leapt off the hills upon the Harbour with the rushing sound of a great saw cutting wood. They were mingled with hail, and when the gust roared past it left the hills white to the sea, as if a mighty smearing hand had passed across their face. The water was hard, and black like iron; but at every snarl when the wind veered into the north-west it suddenly whitened, like iron in a furnace.

Times like these call up every skill of fisherman and seaman if men and boats are to survive. The men go slowly about their work, as the ploughman moved slowly behind his horses; a watching stranger may call them lazy, but let him do their day's work before he speaks.

In any case we are all marked down as 'lazy' – the 'lazy Highlander' is proverbial. Most of our incoming settlers quickly learn 'the crofter's psalm' to quote gleefully:

O that the peats would cut themselves,
The fish jump on the shore,
And I within my bed to lie
Henceforth for evermore!

Perhaps if they had carried a creel of peats on their back off the hill, and sat up baiting deep-lines, and cleaned the catch and humped it to market, they might understand that opening *O that*… but the speech is slow, the rhythm of life is ruled by tide and weather, and there is also a despair at the heart – though that is another matter. (They don't know, either, that the verse is one of many made up for use in metrical psalm practice, so that the holy words themselves were not debased by constant repetitions). No countryman anywhere squanders his strength by rushing at a job; he has hardwon craft, inborn skill, he knows how. Working alone, his life in his own hands under God, he must go surely and see the end in its beginning ('In My End Is my Beginning' says the bed-hanging Mary I of Scots embroidered).

At Tarbert Quay and Tarbert Fair ploughmen and fishermen met, and to them came seafaring merchants and drovers who knew the hill-trails from Kintyre to Falkirk. There is no knowing when those trails were first trodden, no knowing at all who steered the first trading boat into Tarbert. All we can tell is that here, at the crossroads, sea-trails met land-trails, skill met skill and craft met craft.

I was tidying my grandfather's desk one day when I found a packet labelled *Old Coins*. Aha, I thought, I can guess – a Kruger shilling (there it was), a Mexican silver dollar (here we have it), a fat George III penny, a rupee. One twist of paper was marked in his smallest script, and had to be carefully unfolded: "Found by workmen digging foundations for a villa near the East Pier in Tarbert in 1886, and given me by the Doctor. Athenian tetradrachm of c. 490 BC."

And it was.

My hand shook so that I nearly dropped it. A dullish, thick, silver disc, a little bulged by the coiner's stamp, mint-fresh; on one face a sprig of olive and a Little Owl, *Athene noctua*, staring alertly over the letter A Ø E; on the other Pallas Athene herself, mistress of skills, her lips touched with a secret smile. Her hair is bound with a fillet – she had not then acquired her crown

178

of ships' beaks (their absence provides the date).

What else lies below the beached keels, under the fishermen's feet? Who brought that coin (and reportedly eight more), who dropped it in sand three feet below the present surface, who had to leave without it when the shipmen called – ten years before Salamis? All around us the past has fed the present and will feed the future if we draw upon it, but we need to know how to use the great inheritance.

25

But Yesterday

YESTERDAY was summer.

Waking early on a blue May morning to a sound as thrilling as trumpets that stretches on, and on, and on – tumble into clothes and run, run to the gate above the headland and there she is, a little smug black ship close inshore with a white plume at her red funnel. The coalboat's here.

She was a flat-bottomed coaster, designed to waddle ashore on sandy beaches; a puffer. Our shoreline is guarded by reefs, so she anchors off and waits. With her coming everything is reoriented; the school closes, for the children are needed elsewhere. Whatever was planned on the farms must wait; at both ends of the bay carts rumble down grassy tracks, the men standing up despite the lurchings, for nobody can be seen to sit on a shaft. Old ships' boats are launched and poled out, taking the men who have drawn the early stint of shovelling in the hold. John Joiner stands by the weighbridge (we know it as the Wheeze), steel spectacles on his nose, carpenter's pencil at the ready. The coal-ree gates open wide, barely a load left inside from last year's cargo.

The boys have left their boots at home and race barefoot over the machair. It's a law of the Medes and Persians that we 'get our bare feet' from the day the boat comes, though boots must still be carried round the neck and laced on at the school gate. The boys are supposed to be collecting driftwood for noonday fires, but they'll attend to that when they begin to feel ravenous.

By mid-morning mothers and sisters are staggering down bearing big pots of broth, iron kettles, and baskets of crockery. Long before that the deck-cargo is ashore – fencing wire, timber, drain tiles – and the hatches are off.

The boats alongside are loaded gunwale-high with coal and sculled to the beach where the carts back down, one on each side. This is where the boys are needed, to glean the tideline; finders keepers. Some horses are scared of the waves, others are well used to having their great hairy feet bathed in salt water. They plowter up the white sand, halt while John peers at his scales, trundle into the ree to coup their load and out by the other gate. Neighbours' carts work alongside ours; they have a share of the cargo and will take a first load home tonight, coming piecemeal for more as necessary. The main thing is to discharge the ship while the weather holds.

By dinnertime everyone is uniformly black and exhausted, down to small girls in pinafores. The horses drink at the ford and crop the grass; some have brought nosebags and munch their oats with a lofty air. Then the donkey-engine rattles impatiently and we're off again. Late at night, long after bedtime, there may be a ride up home in a cart.

That was how summer started. Then came hay harvest, with the Machine clattering; corn harvest, and teams of women twisting sheaf-bands and stooking, the gate set wide when the last load left the field. Ask why, and the answer would be, "Ach, just so that anyone needing a wee puckle corn knows to go in; " but we have no starving Naomis. The gates are iron, and iron bars out...others.

'The Machine' – there was only one. The lawn mower did not count; it was pulled by an elderly pony in leather boots, not by glossy Clydesdales with feet as big as soup plates. The corn reaper was a sort of Machine, but it did not chatter so engagingly and its whirling arms were sinister; it could not compare.

Nor was the Coalboat to be confused with a Steamer. Steamers had paddles, and cabin fittings polished to gleam like gold, and red plush curtains. The Coalboat was not called *Vital Spark*, but might have been. Para Handy, Dougie the Mate ("If Dougie wass here himself he would tell you"), MacPhail the Engineer and Sunny Jim, were part of the fabric of life; everyone knew them by heart:

"I couldna but be nice to the woman, for she wasna my wife, so I turned a bucket upside doon and gave her a sate." "I'm feeling chust sublime, I'm like the eagle that knew the youth in the Scruptures." It was Para Handy who summed up that third curse, the midge (the other two being the bracken and the Campbells):

"Look at Tighnabruaich! They're that bad there, they'll bate their way through corrugated iron roofs to get at ye! Take Clynder, again, or any place on the Gareloch, and ye'll see the old ones leadin' the young ones round, learnin' them the proper grips. There iss a spachial kind of mudge in Dervaig, in the Isle of Mull, that hass aal the points o' a Poltalloch terrier, even to the black nose and the cocked lugs, and sits up and barks at you."

Winter came gently, yesterday, through bramble-gathering and nut-gathering and Hallowe'en; and after the turn of the year the Ploughing Match, horses groomed to perfection by early lantern-light, red-white-and-blue ribbons for manes and tails of the First Ploughman's pair, green-and-gold for the second; and their rivals came jingling into the yard out of the frosty dark. I've seen twenty pairs together straining up the slope, the gulls wheeling behind them over chocolate furrows. And I've seen the West Loch frozen across, the *Pioneer's* paddles churning up floes, and a circle of a hundred swans – Mute, Whooper and little Bewick's together – roaring round her like the white birds of legend.

The day before yesterday – my grandfather, born in 1844, kept a diary from boyhood and its pages open a door. In childhood he knew an old man who had been reared by an auntie and she could remember 1745; at twelve years old he walked fifteen miles home from Tarbert in under three hours – "Not bad in trowsers!" He helped dig through snowdrifts towards his parents' carriage; far downhill, a lantern bobbed, held by the coachman leading the horses. Inside lay my great-grandfather, unconscious after a stroke, and astern came Great-grandmama, in her crinoline, head down and pushing. So much for wilting Victorian ladies. She made all the butter and cheese and jam, reared nine children, and at sixty still walked the hill path four miles to church rather than have a horse yoked on the Sabbath. She was district nurse and doctor too, as my grandmother and mother had to be in their turn, for the doctor lived fifteen miles away and arrived in a gig; we kept a bedroom ready for him, and stabled his pony. If he were delayed, Grandfather was apt to provide his own ferocious remedies, chlorodyne and brandy, or a laudanum pill; by good luck he never killed anyone – they were tough in those days.

They called him Old Kilberry. This 'Kilberry' thing bothers people today, but it was no sort of snobbery. Farmer or laird took the name of their holding – indeed, under a law of Charles II it formed part of a landholder's surname, necessary where so many shared both first and second names. J. F.

Campbell, younger of Islay, the great folklore collector, was Iain òg Ìle all his days though his father sold their lands; old Alexander MacTavish in a hill farm, retired drover and bane of his laird's life, was Sandy Muilichin. Surnames replaced patronymics as English replaced Gaelic; *mac Thomais* became McTavish and then Thomson, some MacSporrans became Pursells (*sporan* means 'purse'); but still the land owned the people and shared its name with them.

There was scanty land transport. The Crinan Canal was built with the help of James Watt, John Rennie and Thomas Telford – a galaxy of engineers – and with a last echo of the Forty-five, for residual funds from forfeited estates helped to finance it. Queen Victoria sailed along it in a barge drawn by white ponies, while children danced and threw flowers. A few years later, Great-grandmama fell in and was buoyed up by her skirts.

A stage-coach ran between Lochgilphead and Oban. Once it was held up, Wild West fashion, in the gulch of Glen Gallain in the Braes of Lorn, by masked men who made their getaway on the coach-horses. Most people walked: "John Campbell from Craignish arrived this morning; he had walked 56 miles between 7 am yesterday and 5 this morning, stiffish walk for a little fellow like him". (A retired farm manager, he came to approve the young cattle.)

Or else they went by water. Cattle were shipped from Oban in a skiff and swum ashore at Kilberry; travellers rode to Dunmore, intercepted the Islay steamer inward-bound, crossed to East Tarbert for the Glasgow-Ardrishaig boat, went through the Canal on the *Linnet* and took the *Chevalier* from Crinan to Oban.

Tarbert skiffs came to 'try the cod' or – illegally – to trawl for herring. Great-grandfather put his weight behind legalising the trade, and let his boat-house be used by the crews. The habit continued long after trawling was approved, and it was the keenest delight to my father and his brothers to be allowed to join the fishermen, to share their supper and later to curl up in the communal bunk-bed of heather, and hear the songs and stories as the stars swung over Jura.

Grandfather had moments of Victorian autocracy:

Geekie came along on the grey horse going to Clachan to telegraph for a policeman as there was a great row between the Clerk of Works and the joiners who were drunk. I got upon the horse, in my kilt, and rode home where I soon settled the business...

But the same man could drive his cattle fifteen miles, put them into a neighbour's field, then go up to the Big House and dance reels half the night. A small visitor was heard saying, in a shocked voice, "Auntie, that Cattle Man has gone into the dining room with my grandpapa!"

He was a great dancer and judge of Highland dancing, taught by Great-grandpapa who had whistled for his children's reels. Grandpapa did not play himself, but his three sons were pipers. Two started the Pibroch Society, the youngest became a world authority. They had every chance to learn, for famous performers came to stay, and they formed a Kilberry Pipe Band before the Boer War scattered the members.

> *9th Jan 1889*. The announcement of Annie's wedding gave great excitement. In the evening the Pipe music played by Meldrum, Pipe Major 2nd Cameron Highlanders, was *Ho Ro mo Nighean donn bhòidheach, Campbells are coming, Sweet Maid of Glendaruel, Rejected Lover* for Jock, *Persevering Lover* for Joe Dennison, *Because he was a Bonnie Lad, Over the Isles to America* (Joe and Annie were bound for Canada), and *The White Cockade*, at which the usual amount of kissing took place. All the children stayed up until after dinner and danced.

This was to be a 'gentry wedding' in London; local weddings took place, service and all, at night in the big barn, with the bride in black – a satin-and-bugles outfit destined to be her Sunday Best for evermore – and a feast set out on trestle tables and cleared for dancing to follow. Here too the 'castle children' stayed late and danced with their friends. The outside world sometimes intruded. Grandfather, induced to lend his gig to take voters to the poll in Tarbert, was outraged to encounter the borrowers adorned with Liberal rosettes; convinced that Mr Gladstone intended to abolish the monarchy, he recorded furiously that "the Secret Ballot is a great inducement to Lying". Meanwhile at Poltalloch a voter was reporting his experiences:

Wungfield Maalcolm iss a good man and a chenerous man. He sent a cyart to my hoose and he tuk me to the shteamer, and I got my dinner on the shteamer, and a dram. And he tuk me in a cyart to the foting, and I got a dram. And he tuk me back in the shteamer, and I got a dram going home, and a cyart to my hoose. And I foted for Lord Colin!

This is oral memory; it would have confirmed Grandfather's darkest fears. *Is treasa Tuath na Tighearna*, People (Land) is stronger than Master; and not all 'masters' were in harmony with their people. The proprietor of Kilmory, at Lochgilphead, was most often at feud with his own tenantry and with the town. Having had the misfortune to injure a child as he drove along the main street, he was threatened with a suit for compensation by the local worthies and vowed never to set foot in the place again. Accordingly he built a causeway, still visible at low tide, across the loch. When it was finished the Burgh forced him to breach it and restore access to their quay. He next forbade fishermen to dry their nets at his gates; two of them set off and walked to London, located the Duke of Argyll and with his help got 'a paper from a gentleman in the government' confirming that they could dry nets wherever suitable ground existed. A month later they got home, late on a Saturday, and immediately a torchlit procession formed, with a piper, escorting laden waggons to the lawn below the Castle diningroom. There the nets were spread out until the Monday and the point was duly taken.

Old Kilberry would not have pushed into that particular corner, whatever his views on Secret Ballots; but an era died with him. Change swept down like an avalanche on his world and made it as remote as any tale of *Iain òg Ìle's* recording. Yet echoes lingered.

My father was friendly with the Townsleys, nomadic pipers from whom he collected numerous traditional airs and of whom he would say that they had a better right to the land than he had. He came out of a meeting in Inveraray once to find, on the green by the War Memorial, Young Jock Townsley playing *Bha mi aig bhanais* in, surprisingly, jig-time, perhaps because he had a dancer to accompany. I can just remember holding out the pleats of my first kilt and looking up into the dark-bearded face high above me. I doubt if modern children learn setting-steps by the age of four, but I am glad to have danced Jock Townsley's jig.

    Bha là eile ann – that was a different day.

Note

Bha mi aig bhanais air Bhail'Inneraora ('I was at a wedding in the town of Inveraray') is the Gaelic name of the march called in English *The Campbells are Coming.*

Up the Airy Mountain

Up the airy mountain,
Down the rushy glen,
We darena go a-hunting
For fear o' missing men.

> For fear the chance-remembered word,
> The well-remembered smile,
> Should wake a ghost to walk with us
> The dark and bitter mile.

We passed the bitter mile long syne
When first they went away,
But darker yet we trod it out
On a later fearsome day;

> We know not whether they sleep or wake
> but we hear the same birds cry,
> And that is the twist of the sword in our hearts
> That makes us fain to die.

So up the airy mountain,
And down the rocky glen,
We darena go a-hunting
For fear o' the missing men.

> For fear we lose our hardened hearts
> And turn again to tears,
> Across the bar of the steady toil
> And the slow bar of the years.

HMS Cochrane II, *1943*

26

The Simple Life

WHEN SHE comes in from feeding the hens, the house is dark. The days are drawing in, it's black by four o'clock, but she's not needing the light yet. With a fresh peat on the fire and others drying in the open oven, she'll just toast her toes awhile, it's no matter if her old legs wear *breacan-tèine*, the fire-tartan.

Yon's grand peat. Donald her nephew cut them when he was home from sea, and she caught them as he cast them, and showed his children how to set them up to dry. Donald was away before they were ready, but she got them to the roadside herself by degrees, and Neily lifted them with the lorry for her. Her other nephew, the Professor, dug the garden at Easter and lifted the potatoes in his summer vacation, so between peats and tatties she's set up now. The kale's doing fine if the sheep don't break in – she'll manage through the hungry gap of spring if she's spared.

It's a great thing the electricity; the boys insisted she must have it, and certainly it's easier than cleaning the lamps every morning – though she keeps a lamp handy on the windowsill among the geraniums, for fear of these power-cuts you get with a storm. The telly too, that was Iain's present; she's not caring for most of it, unless a royal wedding or maybe the Edinburgh Tattoo, but it's company.

The layby over the way is as good as the telly. You'd not believe the things you hear from the folk that stop – though she wishes they'd not throw their trash over the dyke, a calf could choke with one of these nasty plastic bags. They will be thinking somebody comes round to clear it up, likely, the way they do in the towns. There was a white car with two young ones in it – they were on their way to the island – *mo chreach*, the island I'll not see again! – but that's not what she meant to remember.

They had this big box in the back:

"Well anyway, darling, it's only for five days, and we shan't be completely cut off while we have the colour TV; even if we are living the simple life, we don't want to get hopelessly out of touch."

She wondered then, and she wonders now, if yon thing would work off a battery like the wee radio Angus brought her; if not, they were in for a sair dunt when they found the island hasn't the electricity yet. Maybe they'd find it not just that simple.

She gets up to fill the kettle. It's fine to have a tap; mind how heavy the pails were, coming from the spring? Aye, but it's sweet water, the spring; she draws a pail yet, whiles. Her mother would never have made tea with burn water, though they used to do the washing there on the bank, with the big *coire* on a fire and the sheets spread on the heather.

She'll need to mind and put a white stone on the gatepost in the morning to stop Postie and give him her line for the shops. It's a pity that van stopped coming, but with so many houses empty along the road it's no wonder.

My, but she would like a bit crack with somebody. Neil's wife is awful good about coming to see her, but she hasna the Gaelic, and more and more nowadays it's the Gaelic she wants to speak. The nurse has the Gaelic, a queerlike northern kind; the doctor has none, nor the minister. When old Annag was alive, many's the good crack we had; she was of *An Taobh Eile*, the Other Side, and the Father that came to see her, he had good Gaelic, we would aye pass the time of day.

The house door's open yet; she'll need to shut it soon. Her mother would have thought shame to close it before bedtime, but there weren't the strange people going about in those days. And that minds her of another queerlike thing she heard.

There was a lady going past with a friend, and she was clean wild, she let on there was people spying on her. It seems she was staying in that house she has – Katie Ruadh's house it is – and here did she no leave the outside light burning all night (what for does she need a light outside anyway?). So Duncan, decent man, when he rose to go to the hill early, he went over to see was she needing help, and what did he get but the height of abuse? She's to bring back plants for a quick-growing hedge, she says, and stop them spying. It's to be hoped she never needs a neighbour's help, for it's not Duncan will go to her door again.

And then – oh my, it was a right tear! She rocks herself at the memory.

She'll need to mind and tell Iain; there were these folk at the layby, the lady had one of these high English voices, like as if she was crying on a cow, you couldn't help but hear every word, and she says, says she – oh my!– she says,

"I was afraid I'd have to give up my music when we came here, but then I discovered quite a good little quah in the village, so I joined it."

"What choir is that?" says the man, and him with a panloaf voice himself.

"Oh, just a little quah in the village."

"Is that the one that took the Shield at last year's Modd?" says he, and a *blas* in his mouth, 'Modd'," as if he was speaking about mud on the road, no *mòd* at all.

"Oh," says she with a toss of her head, "that garlic! I don't believe in garlic, when they start that nonsense I just sit down."

Wasn't she the one? I'm thinking she'll not get to go to the competitions, for fear the adjudicator would pick her for the Gaelic test and put the whole jingbang of them out!

Whiles, they'll come to the door and ask if they can 'use the bathroom'; but ach, what can I do but say I've no bathroom nor anything else but the place out the back behind the blackcurrants? Then they'll ask is there a pub down the road? Ladies even, speaking about a public house quite joco; aye, I tell them, there's the inn at the pier but it's fifteen miles. It's sorry I am not to ask them in, my mother would have died before she let any traveller pass the house, but between the price of things now, and no van – and it's aye a Saturday they come, and no chance to get anything until Monday evening – well, I could give them tea, but that's not what they're after when they ask for a public house – and the other I do not have, unless for a cold or at the New Year.

Yon was an awful thing Sandy was telling me, how he was on the hill after a hummel stag that needed to be culled before it left more ugly beasts like itself. He was all day seeking it before he got a chance, and he was down behind a rock with the sights on the beast's shoulder, the first pull taken and him just breathing out to steady himself, when what does he see coming across the sights but a woman's hat with a red toorie on it? I'm telling you, Sandy was fast across that glen! Here she was, her and her wee boy, out with a picnic to try could they see a red deer (but they never saw any until Sandy showed them the hummel making off for the sanctuary). A nice enough woman, Sandy said, and gave him a cup of coffee, but then she began and yoked on him for a murderer.

Sandy was fair dumbfounded. He tried to tell her about the folk that come to the hotel for the stalking, and how they'll only shoot a good head, and he has to cull out the poor ones, the like of yon hornless monster that's away out of range, or a good old stag going back; and the yeld hinds in winter. There'd be no grass for the rest of them, and no royals for the gentlemen, says Sandy, without the numbers were kept in check; and he says,

"Is it the wolves you want back? It's for lack of wolves that there's so many deer, and forbye I kill them clean – better one bullet in the right place than dwining away with hunger, I would say. It's quicker than the old days when they used to chase the deer with dogs into yon elrig down there, yon cleft with the funnel of dykes into it, and fire arrows into the mob."

"Och," says she, "but shooting's cruelty!"

"Aye mebbe, and so's starving. Thank you kindly for the coffee, and don't for any sake be stravaiging the hills again in the month of August without you cry in at my house first till the wife tells you where I'll be, for fear I canna get my finger off the trigger as fast another time."

It's desperate, the ignorance. They're telling me there's folk go swimming under the water, like on the telly, and they'll even lift a lobster out of a creel. You'd think they would know some person had set the creel to make his living, and him out in a wee boat all day and bait-fishing half the night. It's the same as the foreign trawler that put in to Eilean Beag last year. Some of the boys saw her and went to see was she in any trouble, and here did they no get the bold lads at the shore skinning a ewe! Didn't the blagyirds let on they thought she was a wild animal – and her with a lugmark and blue keel on her fleece? They think there's nobody in this place, nobody at all, it's just a playground for themselves.

But it's these cars with the caravans on behind that I don't like. They go fleeing by, *whuff!* and on till they meet something, and then, can they get by? They can not. Neily was saying they should be put through an examination before they were let on these roads, to see could they reverse, and did they understand they were to let other folk past if they wanted just to dander along. It's never in their heads, Neily says, that a body could be going to catch the Glasgow bus or maybe to the surgery, and nothing till next day if he misses. He's thinking maybe they believe 'single track' is the Gaelic for a one-way street; he doesna like the caravans, Neily.

Mind you, it's great how they have everything in these caravans, tins and all. You would think, when they had room to bring them they could take the empty cans away home again, but that's not their style at all. Now me, I've a job getting rid of any rubbish I have, not that there's much when I'm on my own, and I burn what the hens can't eat; it's not to be expected there would be a collection round here, with so few in it, I just put any tins in a poke and Neily coups it some place. He's a good lad, Neily, for a Cameron.

Aye-weel-a-weel! I'll need to be shutting yon door. That's a sharp wee wind, what my father would call a stranger's wind – *is fuar, gaoth nan coimhneach*, 'it's cold, the strangers' wind'. Well, it's all strangers now. They tell me someone has Annag's house bought for a holiday cottage. Annag would have been wild to hear her house cried a 'cottage', a good croft-house and improved forbye. There was none of her folk ever cottars that I heard of, unless yon old man up in Fuarglen, him that wasna quite right, he was some kind of a friend on the mother's side. Well, when they come, it'll be a light I can see from the window.

If they would come to stay all the year, now – if they would be young ones, with a family – maybe the school would be opened and that would save Neily's wee ones going in the bus with the Secondaries. If they were the right kind there's a living to be made off yon croft, it's good land, though the man would likely need a job besides. I wonder would he get anything with the Forestry? Duncan said they were cutting back on labour till the trees come ready for felling.

But maybe it's just for weekends and a fortnight in the summer, that'll no start the van coming. Or, if they do stay, they'll likely no bother with the croft; it's hard work, a croft, and a lot to be learnt; it's all right when you're young.

But why would any young person want to come here? Duncan has his name down for a house over the hill, for when he retires – he'll need to flit some place, for they'll need his house for a shepherd, and with Annag's house sold there's nothing he could get, even suppose he had the money. It's just old done women like myself that'll be left soon, by the few that's still working, like Neily and Duncan himself. Not a man about the place all day – whiles I'm feart, suppose there was a fire, what would I do? –even a wee job like cleaning a gutter, if you need a hand you've to wait until the evening. There's not so much as a boy to run a message. Even her with the hedge, she's no young.

Sighing, she stands at the door. The sough of a long wave travels over the fields, bringing the scent of seawrack. Yon was heavy work, fetching up back-creels of wreck for the potatoes! She shuts out night and memory, clicks down the switch and settles with her knitting in front of the television to see what the world is doing. Around her the treasures of a lifetime's gathering gleam and glow.

My, see yon traffic! Is that London? Poor souls, no wonder they're wanting away; what was it Donald was saying they call it? Aye, a rat's race; just that, like rats in the barn when you shifted the sacks. I would never manage to cross one of thae streets – mercy, will you look at that?

But whiles it comes over me to wonder – how would yon folk manage in the likes of this place?

The Smoky Smirr o' Rain

A misty mornin' doon the shore wi a hushed an' caller air,
an' ne'er a breath frae East or West tie sway the rashes there,
a sweet, sweet scent frae Laggan's birks gaed breathin' on its ane,
their branches hangin' beaded in the smoky smirr o rain.

The hills aroond war silent wi the mist alaang the braes.
The woods war derk an' quiet wi' dewy, glintin' sprays.
The thrushes didna raise for me, as I gaed by alane,
but a wee, wee cheep at passin' in the smoky smirr o rain.

Rock an' stane lay glisterin' on aa the heichs abune.
Cool an' kind an' whisperin' it drifted gently doon,
till hill an' howe war rowed in it, an' land an' sea war gane.
Aa was still an' saft an' silent in the smoky smirr o rain.

George Campbell Hay from Wind on Loch Fyne, *Oliver & Boyd, 1948*

Note
When George gave me permission to reprint this poem he also, and most generously,
sent me his later Gaelic version (first published in *Gairm 67*, 1968) and an
unpublished translation (6 April 1971); and explained that "Am Paiste Beag, the
Little Patch, is a field belonging to the long-deserted farm of Laggan Roaig on the
shore between Tarbert Lochfyne and Skipness". These variations follow; quite apart
from their own merits they illustrate the poet's art in three of his languages. *Soraidh
leat, mo charaid!*

An Ciùran Ceòban Ceò

Dol sìos an cladach madainn dhomh, 's an t-athar ann gun deò;
bha sìth feadh fuinn is mara ann, is taise bho na neòil.
Cha chluinnte feadh a' chiùinis ach fann-chiùcharan aig èoin.
Bha gach nichein tosdach, driùchdach anns a' chiùran cheòban cheò.

Cha robh àird no iùl ann a stiùireadh neach 'na ròd.
Cha robh àit no ùin' ann ach aon chiùineas domhain, mór.
Bha'n saoghal làn de'n mhaoithe fo dhraoidheachd is fo chleòc,
is bann-sìthe air mo shùilean anns a' chiùran cheòban cheò.

Cha n-fhaicte fonn no faire. Bha sàmhchar air gach nì.
Bha beithich agus dùsluingean 'nan smuid gun dàth, gun lìth.
Bha cnuic is glacan paisgte ann, is chailleadh muir is tìr;
Bha fois is clos is dùsal anns a' chiùran cheòban cheò.

Chaidh sliosan agus leathadan á sealladh anns na neòil.
Cha robh dath no fuaim ann, no uair, no solus lò.
Bha'n sileadh mall, rèidh, socrach air cnoc, air glac, air lòn,
is bha'm Paiste Beag fo dheatach anns a' cheathach cheòban cheò.

Bha na ciothan ceathaich chiùranaich, 's iad dùmhail, dlùth, gun ghlòir,
gu cagarsach, go cùbhraidh, tais, ùr, gun ghùth, gun cheòl,
a' snàmh mu mhill is stùcan, 's a' dùnadh mu gach còs.
Bha tlàths is tlachd a' tùirling anns a' chiùran cheòban cheò.

The Smirry Drizzle of Mist

As I went down the shore on a morning, without a breath stirring in the air, there was peace throughout land and sea and a small rain from the clouds. All that could be heard through the still-ness was a faint cheeping of birds. Everything was silent and dewy in the smirry drizzle of mist.

There was no airt or guidance there to direct one on his way. There was no place or time there, but one deep, vast stillness. The world was full of tenderness and happed in a cloak of enchantment; and my eyes were blindfolded by a fairy power in the fine drizzle of mist.

No land or horizon could be seen. Quietness lay over everything. Birch trees and thickets were in a smoke of mist, hueless and colourless. Hills and hollows were enfolded in it, and land and sea were lost. There was peace and rest and slumber in the fine drizzle of mist.

Braes and hill slopes went out of sight among the clouds. There was no colour or sound there, or time of day or light of day. The slow, steady, gentle drifting of smirr was over howe and knowe and loaning, and the Wee Patch was in a smoke in the foggy drizzle of mist.

The thick, close, soundless showers of smirry mist – whispering, fragrant, soft, fresh, without voice or music – were swimming around summits and cliffs and closing in about every hollow. Gentleness and pleasure were drifting down in the smirry drizzle of mist.

27

Tomorrow

MIDWINTER, AND close to midnight; a still and moonless midnight, with a light mist veiling the stars and only the faintest of green glows in the northern airt, so that the bare branches of the ash-tree can just be seen and no more. The dry grass is touched with frost, a roe-deer's hoofs drum briskly as she trots past the house. Far across a bare field the barn-owl sweeps on noiseless wings and sends her eerie cry trembling through the cold air – *Cailleach oidhche*, the Old Woman of the Night, incarnation of an ancient goddess, embodiment of age, winter and wisdom.

The past rushes down out of the darkness – the year that's away, the good things gone; but quicker than old sorrows swoop comes a growing chime of little bells. *Tee*-tu-tu, *tee*-tu-tu, the golden plover fly under the sky-arch, dipping their glinting wings right-left-right as they sweep from the hill. They will drop upon the ridged sea-wrack just at tide-turn, for now through the still air travels a slow sigh, and another, and a third, and with it the crying of wakened gulls. The sigh is like the slow breath of a half-roused sleeper; the land may slumber deep, but never the sea.

Or it may seem that the land is profoundly asleep in these long nights, curled upon itself like a hedgehog in its nest of leaves; but life does not stop when the cold comes. There is still, in the lee of the garden wall, one frost-speckled rose on a bare stem, tattered and scarcely scented, but a rose of the wilderness none the less. Between the knees of a mossy tree root a second primrose unfolds beside the first; the white-tipped arrows of snowdrops stand ready to tilt over and open their dancing bells. There is never a dead halt, never an end to hope.

Now in the depths of winter, when the sun stands at the solstice, comes the time of two-faced Janus whom the Celts also knew. Throughout the Celtic world-that-was strange stone heads are found, carved with two or even three faces, lifesize or smaller. Turn them in your hands, and each is different – one looking back through veiled eyes with a sad smile for bygone follies, another staring wakefully ahead with an enigmatic twist to its lips. *Only a broken old head*...the oracles are dumb; perhaps the right question has not yet been asked. Why should we ask, we who know all the answers?

This is the time for good resolutions and forward planning, a quick glance behind and a long look ahead. It's too late to change the past, but you will hardly frame your New Year resolution without some thought of what went wrong last year. You cannot confront each and every situation afresh with no reference to experience; only a fool can't learn from his mistakes. This is the only justification for recording history. I should be sorry to leave the impression of dwelling on bygones to the exclusion of present and future; I would prefer to see the past used as trees use their fallen leaves, a compost to feed future roots. History has moulded the present and will colour the future of nations as of individuals, whether they study it or not. Only the man who has lost his memory confronts each day in bewilderment, unable to draw upon inherited talent or acquired skill; and even the amnesiac may find his hands moving of themselves in arts he does not know he knew. A nation that ignores its past is in the same sorry case; sorrier still is the case of the country whose history is fed to it through alien minds and the fogs of prejudice.

Shapes seen through mist undergo one of two changes; either they become sinister and dwarfish or luminous and unnaturally tall. Highlanders are constantly presented with one or other of these distortions of themselves and their forebears – even at times both at once. There is the image of 'pestiferous clans' speaking an 'unchristian tongue', dirty and benighted; against it stalks the apparition of the Noble Savage, golden-haired soul of ancient virtue, striding over mountains with a wild song on his lips, untrammelled by work or sickness, loyal and courageous, expressing profound ideas in the language of the Garden of Eden. ("In the islands of Argyll," says MacAlpine's 1847 *Gaelic Dictionary*, "where every word is as Adam spoke it...") Neither of these fictions is much help in daily life, and I can only hope I may have dissolved some of the mists that have nourished them for all too long.

The Noble Savage in his Golden Age is an ancient dream. Hesiod gave it to Greece; it flowed through the Rome of Augustus to the England of St Thomas More, the France of Rousseau. Tacitus wrote a typical Noble-savage speech for his Caledonian fighter Calgacus: "We, the last Men on earth, the last of the free... Yonder stands our enemy...they make a wilderness and call it peace."

Solitudinem faciunt, pacem appellant. For an invention, it has turned out remarkably like a prophecy. The myth of a lost innocence, a serpentless Eden, persists and hides the truth – that savagery is endemic and seldom noble; that Utopia is irony; that the Serpent is securely anchored around the Tree of Knowledge. We are better off with a Gaelic proverb: *tha do dhà chrann air do bhois* – your two lots are on your palm; or even this, *an ràmh a's fhaìsge iomair* – pull the oar that's nearest.

As for the dirty, dwarfish, ignorant hillman – I sometimes feel that we who live among the hills have indeed fallen under enchantment. We are *fo geasa*, under spells, that imprison us within walls of glass. We are trapped in our beautiful landscape, which must be kept exactly 'as it was' (but when?), an exquisite fossil; and fossils are, by definition, dead. Beat as we will against its shell, those who gaze lovingly on it cannot see us. We have become 'People of the Green Hills', living underground among the old dead in the cairns, our music occasionally echoing to the outside world, our cairns sometimes opening to let others dance with us and forget the passing of time; we cannot assert our existence in any terms convincing to that outer world. It would frighten them to think we are not as they imagine – they stand close to us and talk as if we could not hear.

There is nobody there, they say, nobody we can ask about what to do with this place, we must try to invent uses for it – sheep farming, forestry, tourism, superquarries. If there is anyone left there, they must be stupid beyond redemption or they'd have got out long ago. What life could anyone expect in such a place? You couldn't stay there all winter, with nothing to do and nobody to talk to.

Look at their miserable houses, they say – low-roofed, thick-walled, small-windowed; but remember they knew no better, they'd never seen proper brick houses. Let's stop using the gloomy slates and those coarse stones, put in nice picture windows and paint the outside a cheerful pink. When the winter winds come to strip the tiles and encrust the glass with salt, we'll be snug in our city apartments.

Let us, by all means, ensure that any surviving children are got out of this deadly isolation, into bigger schools and larger communities, where they can be fitted for modern life instead of stagnating here and occupying houses that could well make pleasant holiday cottages.

We hammer on the glass wall in vain. There is nobody there, they say, and isn't it beautiful?

The people who used to live in these places, they say, were a feckless lot; they all drifted off overseas, they wouldn't work, they spent their time singing sentimental ballads or else fighting each other. Look at those green ridges, those were their miserable fields; they couldn't be bothered to cultivate better farms.

Who cleared the Canadian forests? we shout, and who was David Livingstone if not a Lismore man? The old people carried manure up to those high fields on their backs, and the sea-wrack too, and dug those furrows with the foot-plough, and reaped with sickles and carried the sheaves down to thresh them with flails; was that laziness? This was good ground and fertile when they worked it, and it was their glen and they belonged to it, whoever might call it his. And they sang as they worked; listen, cannot you hear them?

There's nobody there; isn't it beautiful?

The soldiers came, we shout; they put fire in the thatch while the ships lay off the shore; the sheep came, and Lowland shepherds, and the bracken smothered the furrows. Then the sheep were taken off and sportsmen came instead, for a month or two in what had been harvest time, and it was fashionable to write amusing books about quaint gamekeepers and boatmen. Gradually, as more of them learned to speak properly, there were fewer funny sayings, but one could always invent them. And then there was the 1914 War, and the Depression, and the 1939 War, and trees covered the sheep ground and the grouse moors. The trees are horrible, they say, nasty dull green blankets covering the grazings so that you can't wander over the empty spaces.

The black pines were there before the Sitkas, we shout, and the Sitkas themselves gave work and brought people back to the glens; now the work is mechanised and contracted out, and the forestry houses are let to summer visitors.

There is nobody there; isn't it beautiful, apart from the trees? They had all sorts of weird spooky stories in these places, you know; it's a pity we don't know exactly what these people believed – folk-songs, too, some have been arranged and revived.

If we had a small factory here, we shout, we could employ a dozen people gutting and freezing the catch, and the old pier could be improved for the bigger boats, it would be work for us and food for everyone; we'd need the road widened for the lorries, though. This time it seems they have heard; a fish factory, in this lovely anchorage? Think of the smell, the mess, the traffic! The only people left are vandals, this proves it. If only they weren't here it would be so beautiful.

Solitudinem faciunt

In another time a man could be walking at night and he would hear music coming out of a mound on the moor. If he was brave, he would walk in at the open door with the golden light shining from it, and he would be caught up in the dance and whirl round for a night, as he thought – for a year, or seven years, as the world counted time, while his wife mourned and his children grew. Some stories tell of two or three entering together to join a throng of the laughing, singing, dancing People of the Hills. Now things have changed (though I know a place where walkers still hear the music); instead of one or two strangers, there are more guests than hosts. They push in without waiting for the music, and they re-arrange the room and tell the few people they find that nothing worthwhile is being done. It is not easy to entertain so large a company and one so critical of a household's resources.

It used to be considered foul shame to close the house door in daylight; winter or summer it stood wide, with the device of a peeled stick that could be laid across the step if, for instance, the woman within was changing her dress, or if she had too little food to offer a visitor. Many a traveller has come and sat down in the stranger's seat, immediately inside the entrance, and been made welcome; some have stayed and taken to our ways. Down all the years, prospector or poet, prince or pauper or rebel on the run, his was the place at the fireside and the first bite and sup. If anyone was willing to stay and see how we did things, he was soon caught up into a whirl of activity as strenuous as any Fairy Reel. Even today, when we are few and far apart, if it's not baking for the Women's Rural Institute it's making dumplings for the District Children's Party or soup for tomorrow's gathering of shepherds, and the men are out lifting a neighbour's potatoes or dragging a blown -off roof back into place. As for the evenings, those 'long winter evenings', it is pure good management if the Gaelic Choir practice doesn't clash with the Women's Guild, the Sheepdog Trials Committee with the next parish's Whist Drive, Social and Dance.

Our strength lay, and lies, in the practice of co-operation, the ability to join forces without bellowed orders. 'Man alone is no man', 'house with closed door can't be kept'. And there were also the weaker to be helped; an old woman remembered that in childhood, "We never lacked for fish, because you see my mother was a widow so we always got a share."

Now, shut behind the enchanter's wall, we fight a choking pall of apathy, a sense of helplessness; how can we make our wants known, or – more important – what gifts we could offer the world, if it doesn't believe we exist?

Out on the farthest shore of a province of an offshore island of Europe, we are like grains of corn fallen from a mill, too few to be worth the gathering. But there are others beyond the wall who know about enchanters and about small countries with long histories; there is always the possibility that those few grains could sprout where they lie and yield a useful harvest. There is space here, and scarcely-tapped resources, traditions of mutual help, contract, and respect for skill, free in large measure from the sickly taint of class warfare; and there is an ancient and splendid language with music to lighten the work. Curiously, too, it happens that the language itself is a bridge to those friends beyond the spell, who may yet help to shatter the wall; they can both pronounce it and adapt to its grammar, and it holds few such terrors as *plough through enough dough, chough*!

This is not intended to be sentimental. The Gael is a realist; the notion that he is an airy dreamer is one more distortion of the glass wall's making. We have been too polite, in the past, to argue with imposed assessments of our nature and abilities – if we couldn't get through to our Edinburgh administrators, what chance had we with Westminster? – and now we are in danger of accepting alien verdicts.

"Three things", said an Irish philosopher, "three slender things that sustain the world; the slender green hair of young corn, the slender thread of milk from a cow's udder, and the thin stream of spun wool flowing from a woman's spindle". In the legends it is always a small thing that overcomes, a homely thing that defeats giants or enchanters. It could be that the day of small things is near, coming upon the world in a groundswell rising against superpowers, ant-hill cities, faceless manipulators. Starting from claims of the right to do one's own thing, and from the search for clean air beyond the smoke, a tide begins to set towards the shore of small countries everywhere, where people can be people and not cogs in a machine. The long sigh of tide turn has been heard; we might soon find the three magic rowan berries, the one pebble among all the pebbles in the burn, to shatter the glass wall for good – for everyone's good on Planet Earth.

There are portents to be read in the weather at New Year. If a great round-headed black cloud rises, that is *Tarbh-coille*, the Forest Bull, and signals a year of storms. Once maybe it was an ill omen if aurochs came near the camp, driven by hunger, as today it's a bad sign if the stags come off the hill and go about the gardens. The other omen for New Year, or soon after, is if there comes a little wind off the sea, a westerly with a touch of warmth and a drop of rain in its mouth. All night the dry trees talk and dance, and with morning you see a newness, a hint of rose-madder on the birches, a purplish grape-bloom on the black alder twigs; even old beeches, clinging to their russet leaves, seem to remember spring and the squirrels' races. This night of the kindly wind we call *Dàir na coille*, the Woods' Mating, and it brings the promise of summer and the continuance of the wheeling year. The face of Janus wears a smile.

Dark the night, and more cold coming, yet as I open the door on the stroke of midnight to let out the old year and welcome the new I shall say, as always, to the blackness and whoever may be listening out there:

A good New Year to us – *Bliadhna mhath ùr dhuinn!*

Envoi

'ISLAND YEARS'

for MIC, 27 July 1945,

with a copy of Island Years *by F Fraser Darling*

Two words to wake the bygone years of roaming,
The far-off summers of my childish ease,
When dewy mornings or a rainwashed gloaming
Revealed the glories of the western seas.

Treasures of bird and flower, the welcome Highland,
Spinning-wheel valleys where the peat-reek lies,
Or Fingal's black, Columba's rosy island,
And over all the wide-horizoned skies.

Return our feet no more to see the mountains,
The Holly-leaf, or to MacAskill's door,
Or where the Banner waits, or where faint fountains
Fall drifting from the cliffs to Morvern's shore?

Cha till, cha till – but still our hearts remember
From isle to isle that August days unfold,
Down to the latest thought of last December
When smiled in snow our own proud Hill of Gold.

Book List

Adomnan's Life of Columba; Latin text, tr. and ed. A.O. and M.O. Anderson; Nelson, 1961.

Argyll, an Inventory of the Ancient Monuments: Royal Commission on the Ancient & Historical Mons. of Scotland; 1. *Kintyre*; 2. *Lorn*; 3. *Mull, Tiree, Coll & Northern Argyll*; 4. *Iona*; 5. *Islay, Jura, Colonsay & Oronsay*; 6. *Mid Argyll & Cowal, Prehistoric & Early Historic*; 7. *Mid A. & Cowal, Medieval & Later*; HMSO (1972-1992).

Calder, G. (ed.); *Songs of Duncan Bàn MacIntyre*; Grant, 1912.

Duncan Bàn Macintyre's Ben Dorain, tr. with intro., Iain Crichton Smith; Northern House (Newcastle), 1988.

Fergusson, Sir James of Kilkerran, Bart: *Argyll in the Forty Five*, Faber, 1951; *The White Hind* (essays), Faber 1963.

Gillespie, J. MacDougall Hay; Duckworth 1963.

MacColl, Eòghann/Evan; *Clarsach nam Beann*, 1838; repr. Glasgow 1937; *Poems & Songs; English Poetical Works of*: Toronto 1883; *The Mountain Minstrel*; 2 vols., Gaelic & English, 1836.

Neil Munro; numerous historical novels incl. *The New Road*; *John Splendid*; (writing as 'Hugh Foulis'), *Para Handy*, 1st complete edn. with notes, ed. Osborne & Armstrong, Birlinn Pr., Edinburgh, 1992.

The Horsieman:Memories of a Traveller 1928-1958: Duncan Williamson, Canongate 1994. (Born at Furnace, Loch Fyne, Duncan is an internationally famous tradition-bearer).

Glossary

GAELIC is a language of few irregularities, akin to Latin. There are many teach-yourself books and occasional TV courses. Even without these one can pick up enough to understand placenames. Learners panic over the *ch*-sound, the welter of *h*s and clumps of vowels; *ch* is nearly German *ach*, best sounded as a breathy H (never 'atch' or 'ack'); the letter h was not part of the old Gaelic alphabet and is used to denote 'breathings', better shown by symbols as in other European languages (but it's too late to start that now). The multiple vowels are required by grammar but virtually inaudible. Vowels sound as in French or Italian. *Cn-* is nasal, almost = 'cr'; *le* is liquid, *ll*='ye'; *-nn* deepens the preceding vowel (*donn*='down'); *se,si,*='sheh',shi', both short.

Both *de-* and *te-* can = English 'che' as in 'cheap'. *Bh* = v in 'vale'; *dh*, *gh*, are guttural, *dh* the deeper; *fh* is silent ('); *mh* = v in 'vine'; *sh* and *th* = h in 'hat'. *S* and *T* often = 'sh', 'th'. Adjectives agree with their nouns in number, gender and case, and usually follow them, but some can be placed first for emphasis; *duine sean* = an old man, *seann-duine* = a man of old times.

Abhainn, fem.; *Aa*-ven; river

Achadh, masc,; *Ah*-ha; a field

Allt, m.; ult; a mountain stream

Àrd, m.; arrd; a height, chief
(Àird, adj.; lofty)

Bàn, adj.; (fem. Bhàn); baan, vaan; white (bainne = milk)

Beag, adj.; (fem.Bheag); bec, vec; small

Balach, m.; balah; a boy, 'laddie'

Bealach, m.; *b'yal*-ah; a pass, gorge

Bean, f; (irregular); ben; a wife, woman

Beinn, fem,; (irregular); bain; a peak

Breac, m; brehk; a trout; adj. (Brehk, vrehk), anything speckled, chequered

Buidhe, adj; (fem. bhuidhe); boo-ie, voo-ie; yellow, lucky

Caol, adj.; kyle; narrow

Cille, f.; keel; a cell, shrine, grave

Clach, f; clah; a stone (from pebble

upwards)

Coille, f.; *kee*-ye; a woodland

Dearg, adj.; *jerr*ag; red, scarlet

Donn, adj.; down; brown (and
  surly)

Drochaid, f.; *droh*-hej; a bridge

Druim, m; drim; a backbone, ridge

Dubh, adj.; doo; black

Eas, m.; ess; a waterfall

Fada, adj.; *faa*-da; long (far/boring)

Fear, m; feer; man, husband

Fuar, adj. (fem. fhuar); *foo-a, oo*-a;
  cold

Garbh, adj.; garrav; rough

Geal, adj.; g'yall; white (Gealach =
  the Moon)

Gille, m.; 'ghillie', boy, servant

Glas, adj.; glass; grey/green

Gorm, adj.; gorrum; green/blue

Gualann, f.; *goo*-alun; a shoulder

Lag,m; lac; a hollow

Learg, f.; lairg, a sloping hillside

Liath, adj.; lee-ah; grey

Meadhonach, adj.; *may*-un-uh;
  middle

Mòine, f; *moy*nye; peatmoss, bog
  (A'mhòine, 'the Moss' = a-
  voynye)

Monadh, m,; monnah; heathy
  mountain

Mór, adj; (fem. mhór); more, vore;
  big

Òg, adj.; oke; young

Ruadh, adj.; *roo*-ah; red, rusty

Rubha, Rhu; see next

Rudha,m.; roo-a; a promontory

Srath, m.; strath; a broad valley

Sròn, m.; stron; a nose

Taigh, m; tie; a house (often 'Tigh')

Tiobairt, m.; chippersht; old form of
  next

Tobar, m.; topper; a well, spring

Traigh, f.; try; a seashore

Uaine, adj.; *oo*-Ine; green

Uisge, m.; oosh-ki; water

Ùr, adj.; oor; new

Genealogical Tables

1 Scotland, AD 954-1153

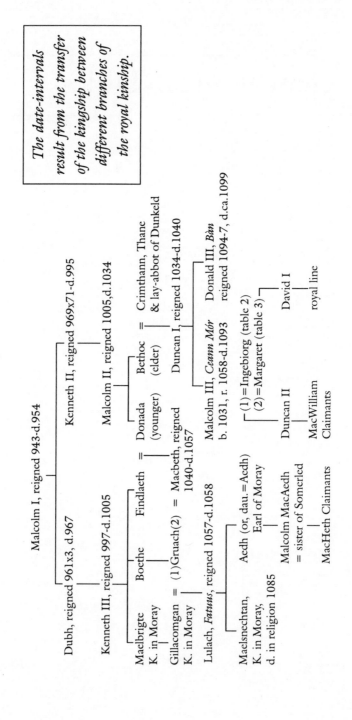

The date-intervals result from the transfer of the kingship between different branches of the royal kinship.

Malcolm I, reigned 943-d.954

Kenneth II, reigned 969x71-d.995

Malcolm II, reigned 1005,d.1034

Dubh, reigned 961x3, d.967

Kenneth III, reigned 997-d.1005

Bethoc (elder) = Crimthann, Thane & lay-abbot of Dunkeld

Donada (younger)

Duncan I, reigned 1034-d.1040

Maelbrigte K. in Moray

Boethe

Findlaech = Donada (younger)

Malcolm III, *Ceann Mór* b. 1031, r. 1058-d.1093

Donald III, *Bàn* reigned 1094-7, d.ca.1099

Gillacomgan = (1)Gruach(2) = Macbeth, reigned K. in Moray 1040-d.1057

(1)=Ingebiorg (table 2)
(2)=Margaret (table 3)

Lulach, *Fatuus*, reigned 1057-d.1058

David I

Duncan II

royal line

Maelsnechtan, K. in Moray; d. in religion 1085

Aedh (or, dau.=Aedh) Earl of Moray

MacWilliam Claimants

Malcolm MacAedh = sister of Somerled

MacHeth Claimants

2 *Norway – Arnassons – Orkney – Scotland*

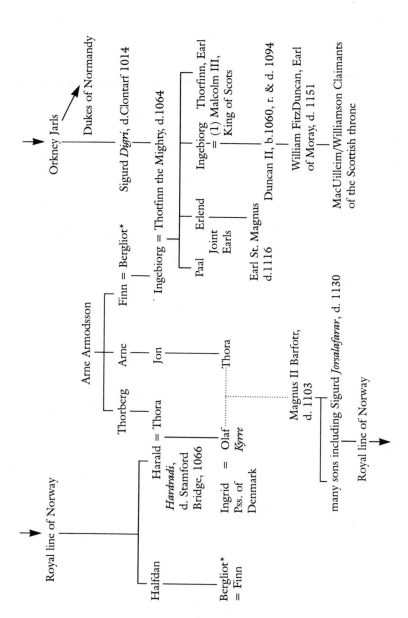

3 Saxon England – Scotland – Norman England

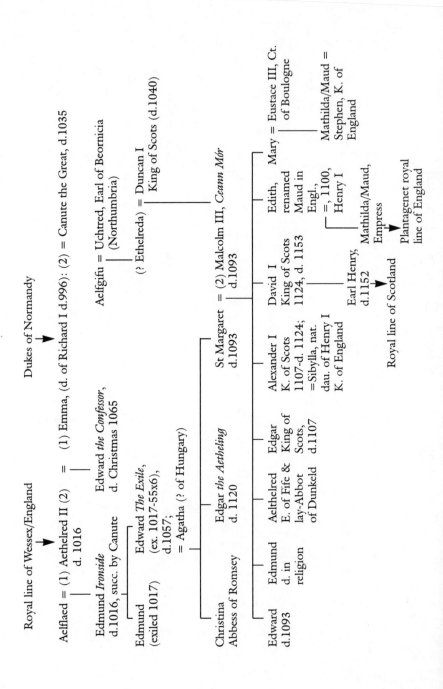

4 *Kings of Scots 1306-1437, with the Earldom of Ross*

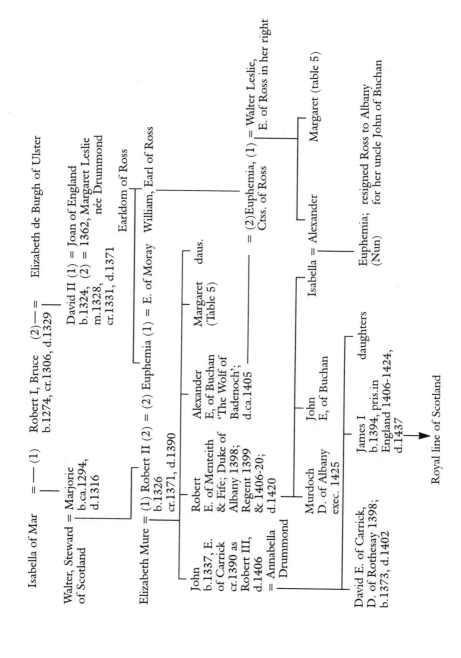

5 Kings (K) and Lords (L) of the Isles, with Kings of Man (KM)

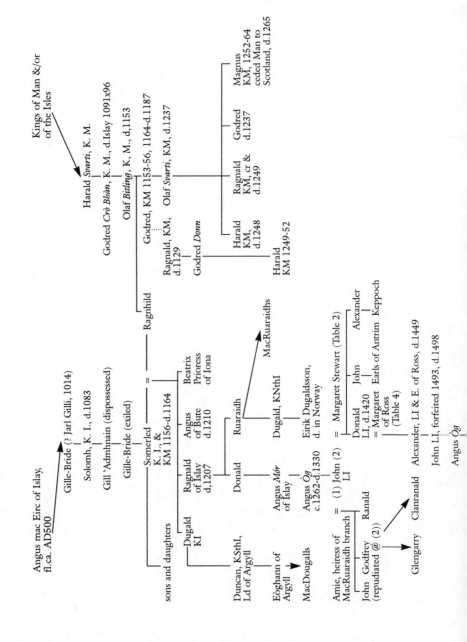

6 Scotland and England 1567-1707; & Great Britain

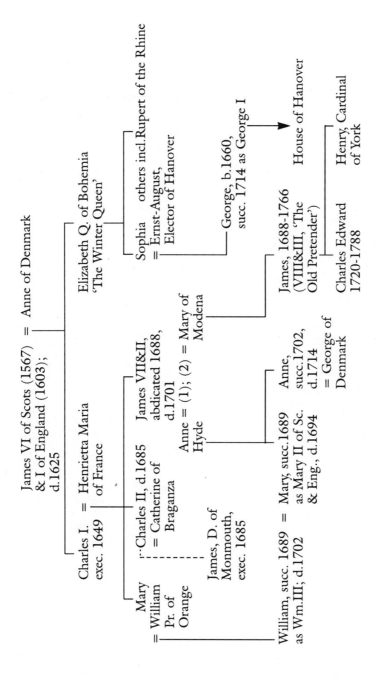

Index